"As we move into a world that promi.... .. .. the physical, Margaret Kerrison is a worthy guide. Her latest book explores how to bridge the realms of games and physical immersive environments in both an inspirational and practical way. Her network of experts and own insights are enlightening."

> — BRUCE VAUGHN, chief creative officer of Walt Disney Imagineering

"Margaret Kerrison opens up a portal between the worlds of gaming and immersive storytelling. This book is a kind of creative sandbox for your mind — providing writers and experience designers with a number of ingredients to play with, dial up/dial down, ponder, reimagine, try on/try out, and then weave into a unique cohesive whole. What's most refreshing about this book is Margaret's unabashed enthusiasm for both the gaming and immersive worlds. Her knowledge, curiosity, and optimism make this book stand out from the pack."

> — BARBARA GROTH, founder and creative director of the Nomadic School of Wonder

"The dedication to 'everyone who plays' sums up the spirit of this book. What Margaret has done with this book is invite everyone into a creative space, to pull apart their work and see where it ticks and sticks, and where it doesn't. This book gives creators the tools and permission to create spaces for people to lose themselves in, to wonder where the time went, and to impatiently seek the next way to engage their body and mind."

> — DIANA WILLIAMS, award-winning producer, CEO & cofounder of Kinetic Energy Entertainment, and chair of the Digital & Interactive board for the Peabody Awards

"With her third book, Margaret Kerrison solidifies her position as a key chronicler in the realm of art and design for narrative immersion. Kerrison insightfully demonstrates how principles from video game design can resonate in real-world environments. This is a must-read for aspiring and seasoned creators alike."

> — JOSH FELDMAN, former executive producer at Xbox, former executive producer at Telltale Games, and adjunct professor of cross-platform storytelling at the USC Annenberg School for Communication and Journalism

"How lucky we are to have Margaret Kerrison to guide us through the wild world of immersive design. With video games as the dominant force in the entertainment industry and an audience hungry for playful experiences, this volume will be useful in the months and years to come."

— KATHRYN YU, cofounder of the Immersive Experience Institute and former executive editor of No Proscenium

"Kerrison, with her considerable and varied expertise, and rich personal journey, offers a unique lens through which to view narrative design, whether you're a writer, game enthusiast, or any creator who appreciates storytelling's power to impact modern lives. Kerrison doesn't just guide you through the intricacies of game-inspired narratives and provide real-world examples of storytelling at work, although that's certainly in here. She also generously invites you into a conceptual world where stories aren't merely told, giving readers the intellectual foundation to understand how stories can be experienced, even lived. *The Art of Immersive Storytelling* is a valuable resource for all storytellers who aspire to transcend conventional boundaries and a testament to the unexplored dynamic potential in the synergy between gaming and storytelling."

— TAYLOR STOERMER, lecturer in Heritage and Museum Studies, Advanced Academic Programs, at Johns Hopkins University

"Margaret's insightful exploration unravels the complexities of story development as she presents a relatable guide, drawing from the rich tapestry of the gaming world and immersive entertainment for writers, designers, and creative minds venturing into immersive experiences, whether they're beginners or seasoned veterans. She demonstrates how the rich storytelling of video games can be a driving force not just for themed entertainment but for any medium seeking the key to success through compelling narratives."

— BRIAN LOO, VP of Operations Development and Exhibition Engineering for Meow Wolf and former Imagineer

THE ART OF

IMMERSIVE STORY TELLING

STRATEGIES FROM
THE GAMING WORLD

MARGARET CHANDRA KERRISON

MICHAEL WIESE PRODUCTIONS

Published by Michael Wiese Productions
12400 Ventura Blvd. #1111
Studio City, CA 91604
(818) 379-8799, (818) 986-3408 (FAX)
mw@mwp.com
www.mwp.com

Cover design by Johnny Ink
Interior design by William Morosi
Copyediting by Karen Krumpak

Manufactured in the United States of America
Copyright © 2024 by Margaret Kerrison
First Printing 2024

Library of Congress Cataloging-in-Publication Data

Names: Kerrison, Margaret Chandra, author.
Title: The art of immersive storytelling : strategies from the gaming world
  / Margaret Kerrison.
Description: 1st edition. | Studio City : Michael Wiese Productions, 2025.
Identifiers: LCCN 2024023763 | ISBN 9781615933617 (trade paperback)
Subjects: LCSH: Authorship. | Storytelling. | Narration (Rhetoric) | Games.
Classification: LCC PN151 .K425 2025 | DDC 808.02--dc23/eng/20240828
LC record available at https://lccn.loc.gov/2024023763

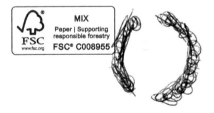

CONTENTS

WHO IS THIS BOOK FOR?

T HIS BOOK IS FOR READERS of my first book, *Immersive Story-telling for Real and Imagined Worlds: A Writer's Guide*, who want to delve deeper into the process of crafting immersive experiences and building worlds in physical spaces and other built environments, especially those who love video games like I do and want to learn how to apply video game storytelling techniques. Why video games? Because they're fun, they help people to escape and experience something completely different from their ordinary lives, and they make people interested in stories and characters in a profound way. They are also some of the best examples of story-telling that exist right now.

Video game stories also invite play, which is a central goal for creating compelling immersive experiences. And so this book is for anyone interested in crafting immersive experiences, whether they play video games or not, who can appreciate the power of play and its value in our everyday lives, in whatever form it takes for them.

This is NOT a book about writing for video games. There are plenty of books on that topic. This isn't one of them. Rather, this is a book about how we can be inspired by video games and learn from them to craft truly immersive, story-driven, participant-centered experiences.

If you're curious about understanding how storytelling in video games can level up your storytelling craft, then this book is for you. In order to create spaces and experiences for people to play, the creator must be a student of play.

This book is for all of you.

For everyone who plays.

FOREWORD BY ALEX McDOWELL

|||||||||||||||||||||||||||||||||||||||||||||||||||||||||||||||||||||||||||||||||||||||||||||||||||||||||||||||||||

W ELCOME TO an ever-evolving landscape of narrative design. World building, as I practice and teach it, is a unique narrative design method, one that lives at the intersection of design, artscience, innovation, technology, story, and narrative design systems. The traditional, linear approach to storytelling, with a single author guiding the narrative, is giving way to a more dynamic and interactive paradigm. This paradigm is encapsulated in the art of world building — a method that transcends the boundaries of conventional storytelling.

As a narrative design practice, world building takes at its core the understanding that storytelling is and has always been essential to human survival, and that as such it is cocreated, evolutionary, and distributed. Linear storytelling, often by a single author and driven by the monomyth, or "hero's journey," is top-down and inert; it does not support the creation of a world as an immersive and interactive resource. This is not to deny that there are magnificent authored stories and worlds, by Tolkien, and Mozart, and Frida Kahlo, and Zaha Hadid, and more, that continue to hold an audience rapt, but they are not spaces of collaboration and change.

There is precedent for this reassessment, in the light of an entropic world too chaotic to be captured anymore by a single author.

> Humankind is facing unprecedented revolutions, all our old stories are crumbling, and no new story has so far emerged to replace them. How can we prepare ourselves and our children for a world of such unprecedented transformations and radical uncertainties?[1]

---

[1] Yuval Noah Harari, *21 Lessons for the 21st Century*.

This book is an exploration of the power of video game storytelling techniques, not just as a form of entertainment but as a revolutionary approach to crafting worlds that invite us all to cocreate, participate, and play.

As you embark on this adventure, consider the notion that storytelling has always been an integral part of our existence, a tool for understanding and navigating the world around us. The concept of world building for immersive experiences, as practiced and taught within these pages, takes storytelling back to its roots, emphasizing cocreation, evolution, and distribution.

Drawing inspiration from the origins of storytelling in early tribes, we recognize the power of shared creation and distribution. These principles transcend time and space, evolving into the great myths and worlds that have shaped our collective imagination. With the advent of the printing press, the dominance of single-author narratives emerged, but now, we return to the roots of storytelling, fostering spaces for cocreation and weaving stories into the very fabric of our worlds.

Narrative space is tremendously powerful because it can carry a massive number of stories, each one with a viewpoint from which the viewer, user, player, or audience can choose to navigate the world. But for that to be possible, the world must be coherent. We can enter a chaotic world, but it is only chaotic in relation to the order that has been the framework of the development of the world.

We live in a holistic world and have learnt from birth how to negotiate it. We are tremendously skilled at this; however complex the system, we don't think twice about walking into a forest or stepping into a metro station or dropping into a new city. When we build a world from scratch, rigorously, we know that the audience can negotiate it, at any level of density and complexity. It only fails if the system we built is not coherent. Building the rules and logic of any world is crucial to its ability to contain and seduce us into full immersion, into a continuing belief in each world's reality.

In a holistic narrative, the design of a well-researched, richly detailed world precedes the emergence of story and becomes a platform for visionary and predictive imagination in any media. Fiction built on deep knowledge allows us to construct a disruptive space for multiple stories to emerge logically, organically, and coherently from the coding of its design. Games and world building are synonymous because they are interactive in creation and experience. The opportunities for choice in game pathways means they are woven and nonlinear and apparently boundless.

A holistic world can be enormous, open, capable of delivering fully immersive experience at multiple scales over years. It's only limited by how much time we are given to build it, and how much knowledge is gathered to inform and populate it. As world builders, those who are ready to take on the task of creating a "powers of 10" container of narrative through time and space, we need to understand a couple of things. The first, and most important, is to return to the historic process of storytelling, which is to accumulate knowledge and harness it. No persistent and evolutionary world that must stay ahead of the demands of its population can do so without provoking many, many sources of expertise in every nook and cranny, which also adapt and evolve as these intricate parts of the world start to challenge each other. The next is to challenge the developing logic of the world at all its intersections by launching stories into it.

Like the "real" world we have lived in all our lives, an infinite number of instances can coexist in time and space, even in extreme conflict or seemingly unaware and isolated. Which means that in a well-constructed world of complex systems, there's no limit to the number of pathways we can take, viewpoints we can own, experiences we can have, characters we can observe or inhabit. When I describe world building as a practice, my hands repetitively define a sphere; the world is not only holistic, it is a spherical container of stories in five dimensions. Each story is articulating its own fifth-dimensional axis through a weave of time and volumetric space.

Our journey doesn't stop here; it extends into the exponential emergence of radical new technologies. We witness the shift from singular author-directed control to dynamic relationships between designed worlds, characters, and the human lens across various media and platforms. This convergence is not just a merging of practices; it's a response to the demands of a new population hungry for diverse, immersive experiences and meaningful stories.

In the chapters that follow, you will discover the art and science behind world building for everyone. This book invites you to become a master storyteller — to embrace the practice of creating narrative containers that transcend time and space. As we unlock the potential of video game storytelling techniques, we embark on a collective journey to shape, share, and play in worlds that captivate our imaginations and redefine the very essence of storytelling.

Let the adventure begin.

— **Alex McDowell**, Royal Designer for Industry, creative director of Experimental.Design, professor at University of Southern California School of Cinematic Arts, and director of World Building Media Lab, World Building Institute

INTRODUCTION

R EADY UP, WRITERS. People are creating and consuming stories like never before. Narratives have become more complex, multi-faceted, emotional, experimental, imaginative, and innovative. The lines between real and fantasy worlds are becoming more and more indistinguishable as we seek to immerse ourselves in the lives and worlds of our favorite characters from beloved games and shows. We want to go into their worlds, walk in their footsteps, complete their missions. But more importantly, we want to make these stories our own. We want to be the protagonists, the heroes of our own journeys.

Playing games allows this in a way that traditional stories don't. It also challenges us in a way that traditional stories don't. It makes us think critically. It helps us build empathy for people unlike ourselves. Games tell stories in worlds that are safe for us to discover and explore. They give us control over a character who fulfills our desire to make choices we wouldn't in our ordinary lives without having to personally experience permanent, dire consequences. It gives us a chance to explore and permission to play, in every sense of the word. Playing games helps us grow our knowledge and perspective.

When I come across a great game, it changes me. As with any good story, it stays with me long after I've played it. Like the first time I played *The Oregon Trail* — it blew my mind. At a young age, it gave me the agency to make decisions like an adult. I was a wagon leader, and based on my decisions, I was going to guide my group along the Oregon Trail in 1848. We hunted, we survived, we died of dysentery. "Learning" came under the guise of playing a game. It had stakes and, therefore, my absolute attention and emotional investment.

I think some of the best storytelling in recent years has come in the form of games. *Animal Crossing* gave me and so many others an escape to a fun, colorful world when I couldn't leave my house during COVID-19 lockdown. *Oxenfree* gave me a sense of adventure while creeping me out. *The Last of Us* made me cry. *Gone Home* made me feel nostalgic for a past I never had. Great storytelling in games can do all of these things and more for the players.

But playing games can also help us as creators. It helps us to appreciate art, graphics, design, storytelling, imagined worlds, and unforgettable characters. Games expand our imaginations, as they did for me as a kid in the form of board games, role-playing games, card games, and video games (whether played on Atari, PC, or Nintendo, or during frequent visits to arcades, thanks to the influence of my hard-core gamer brother). They are engaging, educational, emotional, experimental, exploratory, and evergreen. I call them the 6 Es of Great Storytelling in Games (more on these in chapter 3).

Creators, storytellers, and writers in other industries need to pay attention to storytelling in the gaming industry, especially if they're in the business of creating in-person worlds and physical experiences for participants. People are looking for more ways to engage with stories, not just as passive observers but as active players. As storytellers for physical immersive experiences, you need a strong invitation, an enticing promise, and a replay value as compelling as the content offered by video games that can be played at home.

If you picked up this book, you either understand and appreciate the value of gaming or are curious about how gaming can help you as a writer. If you're not a gamer yet, it's never too late. Many people think that gaming is a waste of time or a pastime for kids. Nothing could be further from the truth. Gaming doesn't necessarily involve having all the time in the world, buying the newest game consoles, or setting up the right gamer environment with fancy gaming chairs or VR (virtual reality) headsets. Gaming simply involves the curiosity to play in different worlds through the perspective of different characters.

As a writer, you need to understand the draw of a great story. You need to understand and appreciate why a great game pulls you back to it again and again, whether for the gameplay, the engaging story, the believable characters, or to finally know "how it ends." A great game makes you think and feel, through action or decision-based storytelling. Find your game and give yourself permission to play. It's one of the best things you can do for yourself as a creator. And if you're a curious creator/storyteller who's always looking to "up their game," then this book is for you.

I consider myself to be a casual gamer, playing mainly for the relaxation, entertainment, and storytelling elements. I mainly play Steam games on my Mac or on my iPhone, iPad, and Nintendo Switch. If you aren't a gamer, or you don't have the confidence to play yourself, watch other people play games. Watching others play can give you insight into the great storytelling and gameplay of different kinds of games. Watch the gameplay walkthroughs on YouTube, which is what I did for *The Last of Us*. I'm not skilled enough to play combat games, but the storytelling hooked me and inspired me as a creator.

The most obvious examples of gaming in immersive experiences are in modern gaming venues like AREA15 (Las Vegas, NV), Two Bit Circus (Los Angeles), Round1 (multiple locations), Joypolis (Tokyo, Japan), and RED° TOKYO TOWER (Tokyo, Japan), where traditional arcade games (for example, pinball and *Pac-Man*) and nontraditional gaming like VR games and embedded gaming in immersive spaces (for example, Meow Wolf) *are* the attraction. Big theme parks like Disney and Universal Studios have embraced attractions heavily influenced by gaming, such as *Millennium Falcon*: Smugglers Run and Super Nintendo World's Mario Kart: Bowser's Challenge. Netflix's Squid Game: The Trials live experience in Los Angeles gave fans the chance to try their luck by competing against one another in a series of IRL (in real life) games complete with cutting-edge technology. These and more are on the ever-growing list of destinations offering live-action and social gaming.

My family racing against each other in RED° TOKYO
TOWER, Tokyo, Japan. Photo by Ed Tang.

Some of these are likely new to you. If you've never heard of it, AREA15 is a reenvisioned "mall" where instead of stores, visitors buy experiences. The website describes their destination as "Las Vegas' newest experiential entertainment district offering live events, immersive activations, monumental art installations, extraordinary design elements, unique retail, bars and eateries, and much more. AREA15 is a wondrous mash-up of experiences and an immersive playground, all rolled up into one vibrant space."[2]

At AREA15, I experienced Meow Wolf's Omega Mart, Illuminarium, and the Lost Spirits Distillery. There are also other experiences, like VR, axe throwing, simulators, AR experiences,

---

[2] https://area15.com/about/

and traditional arcade games. It's worth a visit if you want to imagine what the future of malls could look like.

This is a book about appreciating and learning from video games, not making them, but I'm also excited to see that gaming companies are interested in what we're doing in the immersive experience/theme park space. Following the release of my first book, both Riot Games and Activision Blizzard approached me about sharing insights on immersive storytelling with their teams. Storytellers inspire other storytellers. We support and champion each other, no matter what medium our stories are experienced in. We are fans of all kinds of stories.

I highly recommend that you also read my other books — *Immersive Storytelling for Real and Imagined Worlds: A Writer's Guide* (Michael Wiese Productions, 2022) and *Reimagined Worlds: Narrative Placemaking for People, Play, and Purpose* (ORO Editions, 2024) — in addition to reading this one to understand and set the foundations for immersive storytelling. In *Immersive Storytelling*, I describe the most important questions you must ask before designing any immersive experience. I lay out the craft of immersive storytelling using case studies to show what works, provide storytelling tools and techniques, and explore the essential role of the writer on a complex creative team. In *Reimagined Worlds*, I present a designer's manifesto, compelling designers of environments and experiences to embrace a people-centered approach fueled by intentional narratives. We then delve into the realm of uncharted possibilities, envisioning a world of asking "what if" and "why not" that fosters a deep sense of belonging and authentic expression.

This book will help you to bridge the gap between storytelling and crafting immersive experiences. With insights, examples, and tools inspired by video game narratives, we'll explore how you can create immersive experiences that captivate your participants. Get ready to embark on a quest that will level up your writing skills and transform you into a masterful storyteller.

Let's go.

"We tell ourselves stories in order to live."

— JOAN DIDION, WRITER AND JOURNALIST

A DAY IN DISNEYLAND

IIIIIIIIIIIIIIIIIIIIIIIIIIIIIIIIIIIIIIIIIIIIIIIIIIIIIIIIIIIIIIIIIIIIIIIIIIIIIIIIIIIIIIIIIIIIIIII

I MAGINE YOURSELF walking into Disneyland's main entrance and showing your tickets as you walk through the turnstiles. You see the train station ahead, and you have to decide where you want to go next. Do you go forward to take a picture? Do you turn right or left? Which attractions will you ride first? These are all decisions you make in real time. You might not be conscious of it, but you're preparing your mind and body for play. Disneyland is a destination in which you will give yourself permission to let go, escape, and play with the people that you've come with by stepping into a world of imagination and possibility.

Many of us, especially those working in the immersive experiences industry, imagine our everyday lives as a structured form of play. Isn't life formed by the choices we make and the actions we take? Playing a game is all about choice and action, and the consequences that come from those actions. In the majority of video games, we immediately see those consequences. In real life, the consequences may not come immediately; they are experienced gradually.

Many people come to theme parks and immersive experiences so that they can feel those consequences immediately in their real lives. These locations sit between the fictional world of video games and the daily actions of our real world. We seek that instant gratification, and we go to places like Disneyland time and time again because they are some of the best places to play for all ages. They offer us opportunities to play in different ways with different people in a shared world and context. We can experience how our play influences one another. By engaging in play together, we can feel connected to a larger world.

In our regular lives, we play games in different forms. From board games and sports activities to role-playing games and video games, our gameplay can be educational, entertaining, amusing, and competitive.

In whatever form, games give power and agency to the player. The user is not passively watching, reading, or experiencing a story in a game. Rather, the user becomes an active participant and player in the experience. They are integral to the story, and in some instances, they can influence the outcome of the experience. As in real life, we influence each other through our words and actions.

Playing games also gives us a certain set of rules and parameters that we must abide by in order to achieve our goal. It gives us a clear purpose and objective: Kick the ball into the goal post, find the missing object, vanquish the villain, solve the mystery, escape the room, rescue a character, or beat your opponent. Your participation in the game requires you to be present and in the moment. This is why understanding the concept of gaming is so important in designing immersive experiences.

To be philosophical for a moment, in real life, we often don't know our purpose. We may come close to finding it in our jobs or in our assumed roles in society (e.g., as a parent, student, teacher, boss, engineer, artist, musician, police officer, etc.), but other than our fixed responsibilities within our jobs and societal roles, many of us feel like we don't have a clear objective or purpose in our lives.

When we play games, we have a very clear objective and purpose. We also have a very clear set of rules, roles, and expectations within the confines of the game: We're going to play a certain role on the baseball field. We're going to play a character in a video game with a very clear role and mission. There is no ambiguity. The players, the platform, the rules, and the purpose are clearly laid out for us. Games come with instructions and a roadmap. There is no uncertainty as to who we are and what we are supposed to do.

We all strive for purpose in our lives. With purpose comes meaning, and with meaning comes emotion. Emotion, in turn, moves us to action. When we experience something meaningful, we remember it, and we long to come back to it. It's a feeling of being alive and in the moment, when everything else falls away and we can simply be present. We return to it again and again to recapture that feeling. Some of the best immersive places and experiences accomplish this. It's no mystery why we keep going back to them. By understanding our role and purpose in these locations, we also find our place in the community — a place where we can belong and understand how we are a part of the bigger picture. Never underestimate the importance of our human need to belong and feel connected to the larger world, especially in our increasingly digital age.

With a very clear purpose, we feel a shift in ourselves. We undergo an emotional transformation that doesn't have to be dramatic or life-changing but still causes us to consider our ordinary lives for a moment and perhaps bring an element of the experience or game back to those lives, to remember that we have power and agency in our ordinary lives. That we are the heroes of our own stories and have the ability to change them by taking action.

This is one of the many reasons why we return to Disneyland again and again. When we're there, we are filled with purpose. Whether that purpose is to role-play as a princess or Jedi and feel like we belong in a world that sees us for who we want to be; or to "hit as many rides as possible" within a given time with the people we love; or to check items like going on particular rides, eating a churro, or watching the parade and fireworks off our list of activities. We come to Disneyland with wishes that need to be fulfilled. We subconsciously want to achieve our purpose in our real lives, to make choices and take action based on our needs and desires and immediately feel the consequences.

Video games and immersive spaces like Disneyland give us the unique opportunity to role-play or "try out" a different role or persona, or maybe a more authentic version of ourselves, in a safe setting. We come to these worlds not to be judged, but to feel invited, welcomed, valued, and empowered. They shift our perspectives. They make us feel like we're an important piece of the bigger picture called life.

"We are never more fully alive, more completely ourselves, or more deeply engrossed in anything than when we are playing."

— CHARLES SCHAEFER, PSYCHOLOGIST

2

SHARED ELEMENTS BETWEEN VIDEO GAMES AND IMMERSIVE EXPERIENCES

I REMEMBER THE FIRST TIME I experienced the interactive story-based adventure game *Gone Home*. I made tea, placed it on my night table, and started to play.

> June 7th, 1995. 1:15 AM
>
> You arrive home after a year abroad. You expect your family to greet you, but the house is empty. Something's not right. Where is everyone? And what's happened here? Unravel the mystery for yourself in Gone Home, a story exploration game from The Fullbright Company.
>
> Gone Home is an interactive exploration simulator. Interrogate every detail of a seemingly normal house to discover the story of the people who live there. Open any drawer and door. Pick up objects and examine them to discover clues. Uncover the events of one family's lives by investigating what they've left behind.
>
> Go Home Again.[1]

In this game, I played a very specific character, Kaitlin Greenbriar. She's a twenty-one-year-old who has returned from Europe to the new home her parents and sister recently moved into. There

---

[1] https://gonehome.com/

are clues all over the house regarding what may have caused their disappearance.

I began exploring the various rooms, discovering objects and hidden clues to solve puzzles. Eventually, I looked up from my device and realized that my tea had gone cold. It had been one and a half hours since I placed it there. That's the power of emotional storytelling and engaging gameplay.

You can have participants in your immersive spaces feel just as present and engaged as I did playing *Gone Home*. How? By first understanding the shared elements between video games and immersive experiences.

SHARED ELEMENTS

Venn diagram with "VIDEO GAMES" on the left and "IMMERSIVE EXPERIENCES" on the right. The shared center contains:
- PROMISE
- SUSPENSION OF DISBELIEF
- PARAMETERS
- REWARD SYSTEM
- ROLE-PLAY
- FIRST-PERSON PERSPECTIVE
- PLAYER AGENCY
- SPATIAL AWARENESS
- FLOW STATE

- **Promise:** Participants play to fulfill a promise (wish fulfillment).
- **Suspension of Disbelief:** Participants accept the premises and rules of a fictional world, allowing themselves to become emotionally invested in the narrative or experience despite knowing it's not real.
- **Parameters:** Participants must abide by the world's rules and conditions and the game or space's mechanics.

- **Reward System:** Participants are incentivized and motivated to engage with the game or space by accepting various types of rewards for completing specific tasks, achieving goals, or reaching milestones.
- **Role-Play:** Participants assume a clearly defined role in the context of the world.
- **First-Person Perspective:** Participants experience their own hero's journey through a first-person perspective. Every participant is treated like a main character, the protagonist of a story in which their actions have consequences.
- **Player Agency or Power of Agency:** Participants have agency to choose their own path within the context and boundaries of the story.
- **Spatial Awareness:** Participants have spatial awareness, the ability to perceive and understand their position within the game world or environment.
- **Flow State:** Participants achieve "flow state," a term referring to a state in which individuals are fully engaged in a task to the point where they lose track of time and become deeply involved in the present moment.

Let's explore each of these elements in further detail so we can begin considering how to apply them in our story worlds.

PROMISE

What is the promise, or wish fulfillment?

The wish fulfillment is one of the greatest tools you can use as a creator. What wish does your participant hope to fulfill in your experience? As a creator, you have to clearly define the promise of the story, the world, and the fantasy.

Many creators misunderstand the concept of wish fulfillment. They assume that they have to fulfill the unique wishes of every single participant who enters their experience. As a creator, there is no way you can know what every single participant desires in their hearts and minds. You can't possibly cater to every single individual and grant their wishes. You're not a mind reader, nor are you a magical genie. So you have to set the guest promise. **Setting the guest promise means clearly defining a wish fulfillment *in the context of your world.*** And *this* means doing your research on a subject or intellectual property and fully understanding why any participant would be drawn to that world. Understanding the draw and the fantasy of a story world will help you create the guest promise. That promise fulfills what each guest hopes to feel when they walk into your experience.

For example, when playing *Vader Immortal: A Star Wars VR Series*, the player cannot assume just any character role. They can't decide to play Darth Vader. They play a very clearly defined role as a "smuggler" and captain of a small ship who finds themselves drawn into the events of the *Star Wars* universe. Many story-driven video games don't allow you to play any role you want and fulfill whatever wish you have. You step into a predetermined role in a fixed world with predetermined rules and parameters.

Similarly, when a guest walks into *Star Wars* Launch Bay in a Disney park, they can't assume the role of Darth Vader or any other existing character. They can cosplay, but they can't *be* Darth Vader, because in the context of the world, there is only one Darth Vader. For this world to work and make sense for all visitors, everyone has to abide by the same parameters of the world. There are rules everyone must follow to enjoy the experience.

For both *Vader Immortal* and Launch Bay, then, what is the wish fulfillment? To encounter Darth Vader. To be immersed in his universe. To be in the same room as him and have him see and acknowledge you. For super fans, that is the ultimate wish fulfillment. For casual fans, it's just fun to pretend for a moment and play.

When you set the guest promise, your participants will understand the wish that they're going to fulfill in the context of your world. They set their expectations in anticipation of your experience, hoping that they're going to feel a great sense of fulfill-ment, as if their wishes did come true.

SUSPENSION OF DISBELIEF

What does it mean for a participant to "suspend their disbelief"? Suspension of disbelief is a psychological concept often used in storytelling that refers to the participant's voluntary temporary acceptance or suppression of their skepticism in order to fully engage with and enjoy the experience or work of fiction, even if it contains elements that are unrealistic, fantastical, or exceptional to the ordinary.

In essence, when your participant suspends their disbelief, they are allowing themselves to set aside their doubts and accept the fictional world and its rules as if they were real, despite knowing on some level that they are not. We all do this when we experience works that involve elements like magic, advanced technology, VR, or other fantastical concepts.

In other words, your visitor is openly and willingly allowing themselves to be vulnerable for your experience. They are TRUST-ING you to take them on a journey that is safe, compelling, and engaging. That is a huge responsibility and a great privilege for designers. What will *you* do with your audience's trust?

PARAMETERS

When your participants accept that they will be playing according to the rules and limitations of your world, they also allow themselves to be immersed in the magic, gameplay, story, and environment. Whether they're engaging in a role-playing scenario, exploratory adventure, or any other form of interactive experience, the impor-tance of following the established rules cannot be overstated. This adherence fosters a sense of fairness, competition, and immersion that greatly enhances the overall experience for all participants.

When participants respect the rules, they contribute to a shared narrative or world, making it easier for everyone to suspend their disbelief. This suspension of disbelief then allows everyone to become fully engrossed in the experience as they buy into the established framework and immerse themselves in the fantastical aspects.

When you have multiple participants, the rules and limitations must be clearly and concisely established for everyone to enjoy the experience fairly and equally. Being physically present in a space with other participants changes the gameplay and the social dynamics. The best immersive experiences encourage socialization and connection with other participants. Consider how you can gamify your story to incorporate elements of play and interactivity, and therefore to engage the audience in a more active and participatory way. Blend storytelling with game mechanics to create an immersive and engaging experience for the participants.

REWARD SYSTEM

Many video games incorporate reward systems, whether through points, achievements, or narrative progression. This is a great way to keep players fully engaged and motivated throughout the gameplay. The rewards can come in the form of virtual points or currency that can be used to purchase items and upgrades, or to unlock new content within the game. They can be virtual items or gear like weapons, equipment, or other items that enhance the player's look, with new skins, outfits, or emotes. They can come in the form of leveling up to new stages, unlocking content for new characters or game modes, and collecting achievements or trophies. For example, *Fortnite* offers a Battle Pass system for each season of the game. Players can purchase the Battle Pass, which gives them access to a tiered progression system. By completing challenges, earning experience points (XP), and leveling up, players unlock various rewards such as cosmetic items, emotes, V-Bucks (the in-game currency), and more.

Similarly, many theme parks offer membership or season pass programs that provide guests with various benefits and rewards, which may include unlimited admission for a certain period, discounts on food, merchandise, and experiences within the park, early access to new attractions or events, and special members-only perks. We're also seeing more virtual rewards through mobile apps or games that can be used within the parks. For example, Super Nintendo World's Power-Up Band gives guests the opportunity to collect points throughout the park and in their Mario Kart: Bowser's Challenge ride. *Star Wars*: Galaxy's Edge's augmented reality game *Star Wars*: Batuu Bounty Hunters offers an in-park activity where you can collect points (or "bounty") by finding hidden characters. The in-park app *Star Wars*: Datapad gives guests the chance to dive even deeper into gameplay by translating Aurebesh signs, scanning objects, tuning into and decrypting communications, and hacking devices and droids.

ROLE-PLAY

As we get older, there are fewer opportunities and invitations for us to play. Play is seen as something trivial or "childish." Yet nothing can be further from the truth. When we play, we connect with one another and partake in an activity that doesn't necessarily result in something tangible or productive. We play for the sake of enjoyment. The act of playing encourages imaginative thinking and creativity, problem-solving, and engaging in social group activities to bond with others, build relationships, and strengthen social skills. This social interaction is vital for emotional well-being and a sense of belonging.

Like games, the most successful immersive experiences encourage participants to play, explore, and discover as much as they possibly can. By exploring, they find *more* ways to play, earn rewards, encounter different characters and scenes, and uncover alternative storylines and paths.

A role within a game or experience should be clearly defined so that the participant understands the context of their role within the world. They aren't there to merely observe, so who are they and what *are* they there to do? Be clear in setting their role and objective.

Unlike when playing a game, where a player is given a character (or a choice of characters) to play, most immersive experiences assign roles rather than characters. What's the difference? Many characters in video games are fully fleshed out or developed. They have a history, backstory, preferences, relationships, and set of predetermined characteristics. They are characters who exist outside of our identities.

A participant in an immersive experience, however, is bringing their real selves and identities into the role that they're about to embody. They're assigned a role, but it's much more open to who they already are. In traditional media, participants watch or read the stories of their heroes play out. In immersive experiences, they are stepping into the adventure to discover their *own* hero's story. It's a blend of what's real and imagined, creating an identity and role that are entirely unique to them for the story of the experience.

We, as experience designers, need to create a world and framework where we can "meet them where they are." Instead of assigning them defined characters to play, we can assign a role that is more believable, flexible, and easily understandable: a character in which they can see themselves.

For example, in *Star Wars*: Galaxy's Edge, we gave all guests the same role, as curious travelers to our land, providing them an opportunity to discover the fictional planet of Batuu. They can have different affiliations as a bounty hunter, Jedi, Resistance member, or user of the dark side of the Force, but everyone walks in as visitors to this remote planet. No guest "lives" on the planet. We give all of the guests the same context. They can play a version of themselves within the rules and parameters of the world that we have created as designers. We create the stage in which they can suspend their disbelief.

Star Wars: Galaxy's Edge, Anaheim, CA. Photo by Margaret Kerrison.

FIRST-PERSON PERSPECTIVE

There are many different perspectives in gaming, but the perspective most similar to that of immersive storytelling is first-person gaming. In first-person gaming, you don't see your character's face or body. Sometimes you only see their arms and actions, like picking things up, opening doors, and more. Plenty of games do this so that you can be immersed in the character you're playing. The origin of this first-person gaming perspective stems from our everyday lives, where our own faces and bodies elude direct observation unless we gaze upon our reflections. It's a vantage point we effortlessly connect with. In this perspective, we resonate with the character's thoughts, emotions, and encounters.

Naturally, we bring that same perspective to immersive experiences. In developing the guest experience for *Star Wars*: Galaxy's Edge, I began writing from a first-person perspective to envision each step of the guest's journey. By embodying their experience, I fully immerse myself in their perspective.

Oga's Cantina in *Star Wars*: Galaxy's Edge, Anaheim, CA. Photo by Ed Tang.

When you're creating an immersive or location-based experi-ence, consider how your participant or audience member can be the main character of your story. This is a chance for us, as creators and participants, to step out of ourselves, into a different world and character, to experience a life through someone else's point of view. Some of the most successful immersive experiences strive to tell a story through the participant's perspective.

But that first-person perspective doesn't necessarily apply to just a single role. *Heavy Rain*, a 2010 action-adventure video game, experimented with perspective in a very interesting way. The game features four protagonists involved with the mystery of the Origami Killer, a serial killer who uses rainfall to drown their vic-tims. To my surprise, I got to play all four protagonists, trying to solve the mystery of the murders through the eyes of a father, a pri-vate eye, an FBI agent, and a photojournalist. Transitioning from one character to the next gave me a holistic view of the story, see-ing the case and story from multiple perspectives. It was riveting, and I couldn't stop playing because I wanted to uncover who the killer was. I was emotionally invested in the outcome of the story and the characters I was playing.

We see this idea of alternate viewpoints explored as a trend in classic fairy tales. What if the story was told through the eyes of the villain? That's what Disney did with *Maleficent*, the live-action retelling of Walt Disney's 1959 animated film *Sleeping Beauty* (itself an adaptation of Charles Perrault's 1697 fairy tale of the same title) that tells the story from the perspective of the "evil" fairy.

Consider the perspective of your participant and develop a narrative that will powerfully resonate with them to add depth to your story's context and meaning.

PLAYER AGENCY OR POWER OF AGENCY

The concept of player agency — the player's ability to influence and shape the game's outcome — should be a priority in creating any immersive experience. People want to feel in control and have agency over their actions so they can experience consequences in a safe way. This permission to play is what we are all seeking in our lives.

Consider how to craft story worlds, character perspectives, and plotlines that allow audiences to make choices that impact the story's direction and immerse them in the narrative. Through enveloping their senses in a captivating narrative driven by their personal agency, their emotional involvement deepens, intensifying the stakes at play. The repercussions of their choices are thus more likely to be *felt*.

A "felt experience" is the individual's inner sense or awareness of what they are experiencing at any given moment. It can also include the suspension of disbelief, the willing and conscious avoidance of reality so that one can believe their imagined surroundings for the sake of enjoying its narrative. In other words, the best games and immersive experiences make you feel like you have real choices to make even as you're being guided in a specific direction, with some of the parameters fading into the background of our consciousness once the basic premise is established and we've suspended our disbelief.

SPATIAL AWARENESS

"Spatial awareness," also called "sense of presence," refers to a player/participant's ability to perceive and understand their position within the game world or environment. This is a very important element that many designers overlook. The participant's ability to understand and appreciate the perception of distance, scale, depth, and overall spatial relationships within the space influences how much they believe they are "really there." Achieving a strong sense of spatial awareness is crucial for creating an immersive and engaging experience, especially in VR and other immersive technologies. When something "feels off" in the space experienced by the participants, the immersion is broken or interrupted. It no longer feels real, and they no longer suspend their disbelief. How a space *feels* is directly connected with how it *looks*.

I've played many VR games with my son, but my favorites are the ones in which we can move around in a physical stage with actual walls, objects, and tools to interact with. I think of Dreamscape Immersive's *Curse of the Lost Pearl*, where I was separated from my son and held a "torch" to walk through dark tunnels and solve puzzles to reunite with him. Or The Void's creepy Ghostbusters: Dimension, where we found ourselves in a small New York City apartment before all hell broke loose and we had to use our "proton packs" to eliminate the ghosts. This type of interactive, immersive gameplay successfully uses the space around the player to help add to the believability of "being there" as we see environments, characters, and objects that might not really "be there."

Walt Disney was a master at playing with a visitor's spatial awareness. He and his Imagineers used "forced perspective" to build many of the buildings in Disneyland, a clever artistic technique used in architecture and design to create an optical illusion that makes objects appear larger, smaller, farther away, or closer than they actually are. This technique has been widely used in various theme parks and public spaces to enhance the visual experience of visitors and to create a sense of scale in a limited space. Two prominent examples of forced perspective in Disneyland are Main Street and Sleeping Beauty Castle. By manipulating the size and scale of a building based on the position it will be viewed from, the designs trick the eye and make the buildings and street feel more substantial than their physical dimensions. These tweaks create a feeling of grandeur as guests walk into the park.

Main Street Disneyland, Anaheim, CA. Photo by Ed Tang.

FLOW STATE

How does time seem to fly by when you're enjoying a good game or immersive experience? There are many physical experiences in which I lose track of time and am highly attentive to the present moment because my mind and body are engaged. We can attribute this phenomenon to a combination of psychological and neurological factors.

Both video games and immersive experiences have the potential to induce a state of flow. Flow is a psychological concept coined by Mihaly Csikszentmihalyi describing a mental state in which a person is fully immersed in an activity, feeling energized and focused and enjoying the process.[2] In this state, time perception can become distorted, and individuals may lose track of the passage of time. When your mind is fully engaged and focused on the task at hand, you become less aware of external time cues. This heightened attention contributes to time seeming to pass quickly, like when I played *Gone Home*.

The best experiences make you feel present and "in the moment."

Hopefully, you've experienced this in your life. When you're enjoying yourself so much that everything else fades away and you're experiencing the present moment without worrying about what came before and what will come after.

This is the goal of every immersive storyteller: to create a story world in which our guests are present and simply *feel*. Ultimately, it's capturing the human experience. We go to these places so that we can feel human again.

Felt experiences, referring to subjective, personal, and often emotional or sensory perceptions of an event, situation, or phenomenon encompass a wide range of human experiences, including emotions like joy, sadness, disgust, fear, or anger, as well as physical sensations such as pain, pleasure, warmth, or cold. They can

---

[2] https://www.cgu.edu/people/mihaly-csikszentmihalyi/

also involve more complex states of mind, like love, empathy, nostalgia, or contentment. Each person's felt experience is unique and influenced by their thoughts, beliefs, and memories and the context in which the experience occurs.

After all, if content is king, then context is queen. Content doesn't mean much without context. They need each other. When you place content in different contexts, it holds different meanings.

Understanding and acknowledging the significance of felt experiences is crucial in creating an immersive experience because it helps individuals process their emotions and make sense of them. The concept of felt experience is often examined when exploring questions about consciousness, qualia (the subjective properties of experiences), and the nature of subjective reality. In other words, it's what we *believe* something is like, our subjective interpretation of the taste of an apple or the color of the sky, rather than the definition of *what is*. And isn't life one big subjective experience?

Our feelings improve our ability to predict, learn, and relearn stimuli and situations in the environment based on previous experiences. With our feelings, we assign certain values to different situations and environments, honing our sense of its safety, priority, approachability, and personality. We determine whether these experiences are places we want to return to again (or not).

The process of feeling emotions, comprehending their significance, and attributing meaning to them for subsequent scenarios is a survival strategy that has developed within us since our earliest days. As humans, we acquire the understanding that certain circumstances carry significant implications. Although we no longer face the threat of a saber-toothed tiger, the fight-or-flight response remains deeply rooted within us. This is one of a number of reasons why many of us are attracted to survival games like *The Walking Dead* and *The Last of Us*. We practice this natural instinct of ours to survive at all costs.

• • •

In essence, games and immersive experiences serve as more than mere entertainment; they offer us a gateway to experimentation, exploration, and discovery. Through these mediums, we venture into uncharted territories, unraveling mysteries and testing our limits in a secure environment. It's a playground for the mind, where we can push boundaries, learn, and grow without fear of real-world consequences. Ultimately, this journey of play and experimentation isn't just about escapism; it's about understanding both the world and ourselves on a deeper level.

JUMP-STARTER QUESTIONS

- What is your story about? In other words, what's the theme?
- Why is your story set in this world? What is the world you're creating? Consider the mood, tone, and genre.
- Who is your participant? What role are they going to play in your experience? How will you meet them where they are? Will they want to be a part of your story?

3

THE 6 Es OF GREAT
STORYTELLING IN GAMES

|||||||||||||||||||||||||||||||||||||||||||||||||||||||||||||||||||||||||||||||||||||||||||||||||||||||||||||||

WE PLAY GAMES FOR MANY REASONS, but the best games demonstrate what I call the 6 Es of Great Storytelling.

THE 6 Es OF GREAT
STORYTELLING IN GAMES

01	ENGAGING
02	EXPERIMENTAL
03	EDUCATIONAL
04	EXPLORATORY
05	EMOTIONAL
06	EVERGREEN

ENGAGING

Great games are engaging. That's a no-brainer. There isn't much point in playing a game if it doesn't engage you. But what does it mean to be engaged? Simply put, it means to be interested and committed to something. We are all so distracted, and our attention spans are getting shorter and shorter. As I mentioned earlier, the best immersive experiences captivate their participants and hold their attention. Participants are so engaged in the moment that they choose to be in that world and fulfill their desire. They have a hyperawareness that they don't normally have or practice in their regular lives.

So, what is your invitation to play? Lean into what makes your participants want to play and engage in a way that is rooted in the character, story, and fantasy. Is their goal to be curious? Is it to solve a mystery? Is it to discover a new world?

Think about your participants' actions as "verbs" that will engage them as they experience your story. For example, here are some of the verbs a player experiences in the following games:

- *Tomb Raider*: Explore, discover, solve puzzles, navigate hostile environments filled with traps and obstacles, and fight enemies.
- *Super Mario Bros. Wonder*: Explore, discover new worlds, collect badges and power-ups, avoid obstacles, vanquish "bad guys," and help your friends.

Video games are all about the player/character's actions. When you think of your immersive experience, consider how your participant can do more than just see, read, or listen. Consider how they can engage in the story of your world by inviting them to take action in a way that's unlike what they might do in their ordinary world. Invite them to use their whole bodies to experience your place. Create opportunities for them to discover a new side of themselves by offering activities that they wouldn't normally pursue in their regular lives. By giving them opportunities to do something unique and different, the experience becomes much more memorable.

Whatever the engagement is, it should feel organic and authentic. It's probably rooted in something you feel as the creator. And if you can't find your affinity to the story or world, then invite others who can to help you. Listen and learn from them, and perhaps you can take one step closer to offering activities that will engage your participants.

Ultimately, remember: Never design an experience that you wouldn't want to engage in yourself.

EXPERIMENTAL

"By nature I'm an experimenter. To this day, I don't believe in sequels. I can't follow popular cycles. I have to move on to new things. So with the success of Mickey, I was determined to diversify."

— WALT DISNEY

I love games that are bold and experimental. Whether they're experimental in the format of the gameplay or the storytelling medium or both, I want to experience stories told in unique ways. It opens up my imagination to impossible things. I've played games that use different player perspectives: first person, third person, and top-down (often referred to as isometric). I also enjoy playing games that experiment with different genres, game mechanics, and world rules.

With games, you have the ability to experiment with time, like in the episodic adventure game *Life Is Strange*. You play a character named Max who can stop and rewind time, which makes for a very interesting adventure as you navigate growing up with this superpower. Talk about a game that leans into wish fulfillment! I don't know how many times I wish I could've stopped and rewound time in my teenage years. The game also has a nice handprinted style that feels unique amidst the styles of many modern games.

Twelve Minutes is another interesting game that experiments with time, in a manner similar to the movie *Groundhog Day*. With each play, you have twelve minutes to solve the scene before "something bad" happens (I won't spoil it for you). Time repeats itself over and over again, until you find your way out of the room by solving the challenge. There can be different outcomes based on what you do, but there's a sense of urgency that feels exciting. Also, it's experimental in its use of the top-down perspective of the game. You get to see the room from a bird's-eye perspective so that you can strategize and plan your actions based on the placement of things and people.

Gaming expands the possibilities in storytelling beyond the linear. But what does it mean to experiment with the participant experience in immersive spaces like gaming does with the player experience? Just like in gaming, there are some great examples of experimental storytelling in physical immersive experiences.

In *Star Wars*: Galactic Starcruiser, participants entered as themselves, travelers from their "home planets." Throughout the course of the voyage, they were encouraged to choose allegiances and take action based on which characters they side with. The entire attraction was a bold experiment that gave participants the permission to play with each other in the context of the *Star Wars* universe.

There are also immersive VR experiences like Dreamscape and The Void. These examples are a direct application of gaming experienced IRL. The participants are players in a gamelike, virtual world where they explore and fulfill a mission. The Void did a great job of not only immersing you in a story world, but also encouraging you to work as a team with other participants. It was one big experiment in how a physical experience can be story-driven, game-based, social, and fun.

In playing The Void's *Jumanji: Reverse the Curse*, each member of our group chose a card randomly to determine which unique character we would play. Based on our characters, we had different sets of abilities that would come in handy during the adventure: My character could read illegible hieroglyphics, my son's character was the "muscle" of the group, and another member played the character who could "communicate with the animals." We traversed the precarious trail together, worked together to solve puzzles, and had a good laugh at certain moments of the game.

Some companies are getting experimental with AR (augmented reality) and finding ways to use technology so participants can interact with physical elements in their places. During my time at Walt Disney Imagineering, I worked with a small talented team to develop *Star Wars*: Batuu Bounty Hunters, an AR game that lets you become a bounty hunter and go on quests in the physical themed land. Using MagicBand+ (Disney's plastic RFID bracelet) as your guide, you seek virtual bounties hidden across Black Spire Outpost in *Star Wars*: Galaxy's Edge.

First, you're assigned a bounty at a job board in the land. Then you'll search for the bounty as vibrations and lights on your MagicBand+ help guide you down the right path. When you find your bounty, you can use the Play Disney Parks app's AR "thermal viewer" to reveal who's hiding in the shadows. It's a really fun way to unlock hidden surprises in a unique, interactive way, and it also requires the participant to physically be in the park.

Star Wars: Galaxy's Edge, Disneyland, Anaheim, CA. Photo by Margaret Kerrison.

The Autry Museum of the American West, Los Angeles, CA. Photos by Margaret Kerrison.

If you don't want to consider AR or it's not a viable option, you can utilize other forms of media to add more content to your experience. In my recent visit to the Autry Museum of the American West in Los Angeles, California, I encountered simple, clever ways that the museum used media to bring their spaces to life. It doesn't have to be a mission-based game for it to be engaging. The museum simply used a projector to display an artist talking about the role of religion in his artwork.

When I go to museums, I often wonder about the origin or context behind a work of art. Having these projected images of artists talking about their work is an effective solution. It's also a great way to bring life and humanity into otherwise quiet, nondynamic spaces. Many participants, especially kids, aren't interested in just "looking" at objects and reading text about them. How can you find ways to make them engaged by experimenting with your medium and participant experience? How can you experiment with your storytelling to immerse them in a specific time and place (real or imagined), to create interest by raising the stakes of the story with a clear beginning, middle, and end, and to envelop all of their senses in your world?

There was one room in the Autry Museum where I imagined an exciting Wild West saloon scene playing out. The room had magnificent historic furniture and objects like a beautiful wood-carved bar counter, a gambling table, and other unique items. It's unfortunate that all I could do as a participant was look at the objects and listen to the piano music playing over the speakers.

I imagined going back in time. What could it look, sound, and feel like if the museum added some furniture along with the historic objects that allowed the participant to sit for a short, looped media show set in that time period? Using timed and well-placed lighting on certain chairs, the bar, and the piano and a voiceover of characters talking to each other, the space could really come alive with a dynamic programmed story scene, without the use of any live performers, audio-animatronics, or even an employee hosting the show.

Then I imagined how I might become a part of that story. Could the characters acknowledge that I'm sitting on a chair and draw me into the story in an engaging way? Would I have a small role to play? Experimenting with immersive techniques in different settings can do so much for drawing in otherwise passive observers.

EDUCATIONAL

Many of the games I enjoy don't necessarily prioritize educational content, but I find that their stories play a significant role in my learning process. Stories have a unique ability to teach and imprint information in our minds, helping us grasp the context of various subjects. While I play games for their entertainment value, I frequently find myself gaining insights and knowledge through their engaging storytelling. These experiences not only broaden my understanding of the world but also offer moments of self-reflection. The power of storytelling lies in its capacity to transport us to realms, both real and imagined, across any era or circumstance. It's not about formal education; rather, it's about the subtle ways games open our minds and prepare us to absorb new ideas and perspectives.

I mentioned playing *The Oregon Trail* as a kid, but I also remember as a teenager playing *Titanic: Adventure Out of Time* (1996), which takes place in a virtual representation of the RMS *Titanic*. I played the role of a British spy sent back in time to the fateful night of the *Titanic*'s sinking who must complete a previously failed mission to prevent World War I, the Russian Revolution, and World War II from occurring. It was an adventure game that fulfilled my wish to explore the ship in addition to solving puzzles. Based on the decisions I made, the items I used, and the characters I interacted with, there were multiple outcomes and endings. I loved the nonlinearity of the storytelling and the ability to explore the iconic ship. Additionally, I learned about the *Titanic* in the context of world history. In one of my gameplay's endings,

Adolf Hitler became a famous artist, preventing him from becoming a leader in the Nazi Party.

Playing games gives us the power of agency, allowing us to fulfill our desires in ways otherwise impossible. Through gaming, we can embody the roles of race car drivers, drummers, dancers, soccer players, explorers, or even demon slayers, experiencing these

Round1 Bowling & Amusement, Burbank, CA. Photos by Margaret Kerrison.

fantasies firsthand. It's a platform through which we step into the shoes of others, immersing ourselves in their lives, if only for a moment. In the realm of gaming, we engage in role-play, enact the actions inherent to each role, and essentially take a "test run" to gauge our performance, all within the safety of a playful environment. This echoes back to our childhoods, when play served as a fundamental tool for learning and understanding the world. Through play, we honed our talents and skills, fostering a sense of self-esteem and identity. Games continue to be a medium through which we explore, learn, and reaffirm our sense of self.

While education is often a byproduct of exploring immersive spaces rather than the priority, I can imagine museums and cultural institutions taking a page out of games to make history fun and compelling as visitors learn. It's amazing how when your participant has a role to play and is invested in the outcome of the story, they are more engaged. It can be as simple as assigning a role or character for your participant to inhabit throughout the exhibition or experience, making decisions to determine their outcome. Or it can be even simpler, a participant assigned a historical character to follow throughout the experience so that they have someone to identify with and root for.

Companies like Dreamscape have started dabbling with education in gaming by partnering with Arizona State University to create Dreamscape Learn. According to the ASU website: "Dreamscape Learn is a collaborative venture between Dreamscape Immersive and Arizona State University, merging the most advanced pedagogy with the entertainment industry's best emotional storytelling. Dreamscape Learn redefines how we teach and learn in the 21st century, while aiming to eliminate student learning gaps."[3] Debuting with their biology program, Neo Bio, the personalized curriculum combines skills-based lessons with the narrative-driven Dreamscape Learn VR lab experiences and will

---

[3] https://dreamscapelearn.asu.edu/

use "an adaptive learning platform, which constantly tests students and allows them to review and reinforce any skills that were not mastered before proceeding."[4]

Another example of the use of gaming storytelling techniques in education is the work by the World Building Media Lab (WbML), directed by award-winning designer and University of Southern California professor Alex McDowell. WbML is leveraging technology to enhance storytelling experiences. Collaborating with various partners, they explore how cinematic storytelling principles can enrich immersive experiences. The lab believes in the synergy between technology and narrative, continually seeking to expand the boundaries of storytelling.[5] I can't think of a better way to teach someone about complex materials than through immersive gaming.

In my visit to the WbML, Alex and his team shared their work "World in a Cell," a collaboration with the Bridge Institute, to create a fully experiential virtual world of a single pancreatic beta cell using the metaphor of the complex systems of a city. Their goal is "to use storytelling and world building to immerse both the layperson and expert and engage them in levels of detail that are both scientifically accurate and approachable."[6]

Using VR, I experienced a rich world inside the cell and experienced a mesmerizing, almost meditative journey, as if I were underwater. I floated around this biological world and learned about the complex system of a pancreatic beta cell in a gamified way that gave me agency to explore.

Another example of gaming storytelling techniques in education is the Planet Word Museum in Washington, DC, which employs various strategies to engage visitors through fun, interactivity, and gamification while educating them about language and communication. I thoroughly enjoyed visiting this museum with my son, teen

---

[4] Faller, "New Personalized Biology Curriculum," https://news.asu.edu/20230210-university-news-new-personalized-biology-curriculum-prioritizes-student-success

[5] https://worldbuilding.usc.edu/about-wbml/

[6] https://worldbuilding.usc.edu/projects/worldinacell/

nephew, and husband. Everyone was engaged not only with the interactive exhibits but, more importantly, with each other. It would be easy to add some media screens and call it a day, but Planet Word sought to practice what they preach: They not only want to teach visitors about the art of language and communication, they employ

Planet Word Museum, Washington, DC. Photos by Margaret Kerrison.

effective communication techniques to engage you, no matter what age you are. Everything from learning about the words you sing in a song in an interactive karaoke room, to sitting down across from someone and telling jokes to make the other person laugh, to learning how to pronounce words in Gaelic or Dothraki. Throughout the museum, its designers incorporated elements of gamification into their exhibits and educational programs to make learning feel like play. They involved challenges using graphic props, quizzes, puzzles, and scavenger hunts that encouraged visitors to explore and discover information at their own pace. I was impressed by how they offered many opportunities for visitors to personalize their museum experience, from choosing what language they want to learn to trying their hand at writing clever ad copy.

I can also imagine a world where AI helps build upon a participant's learning. With every visit, a participant could unlock a new level of learning based on what they've accomplished in their prior visits. Based on the participant's preferred subject matter, modes of learning, and pace at which they learn, AI could enhance their experience with each visit.

After the visit, perhaps they could continue their learning at home, in the guise of a game they play online. Yet after playing online, would they return to the physical location to unlock new characters, items, levels, or games? There has to be an incentive for them to return in person. Maybe they would return because of an in-person social event (like an in-story celebration of some kind), to meet characters, to purchase themed food and drink or exclusive merchandise, or to participate in esports tournaments (a form of competition using video games). Even when learning is the key takeaway, it can't be the main call to action for participants to stay engaged.

EXPLORATORY

The best games use their environments to encourage players to explore their surroundings. This is one of the ways even noneducational games allow players the opportunity to learn. That's one of the many reasons why participatory immersive theater experiences like *Sleep No More* resonate with so many visitors. Personally, it fulfills my wish of becoming a faceless spirit wandering from place to place, observing people without being told what to do or where to go. I can simply choose my own path as I explore and discover new spaces.

There are many video games that encourage exploration to unravel a story. Many of them even have virtual museums for you to explore. *Fortnite* launched a virtual museum dedicated to the Holocaust called Voices of the Forgotten in August of 2023 "created by the Los Angeles-based game designer Luc Bernard, with approval from Fortnite's publisher Epic Games."[7]

In *The Last of Us*, players explore an abandoned Wyoming Museum of Science and History as Joel, the primary playable character for the game. You can enter every room, read all the museum labels, look at different objects, and take as much time as you want perusing the space.

In *Animal Crossing*, one of my favorite activities is collecting items such as bugs, fish, sea creatures, artwork, and fossils for the museum. As a designer, it fulfills my desire to see a museum come to life. You can take as much time as you like exploring the museum and enjoying all of the items you've collected over your many adventures.

In *Unpacking*, a nominee for the Peabody Immersive & Interactive Award, "this zen puzzle game transforms the mundane experience of unpacking items out of boxes after a move into an extraordinary storytelling device, allowing the player to get to

---

[7] Meier, "Fortnite's Holocaust museum," https://www.theartnewspaper.com/2023/10/02/fort-
nites-holocaust-museum-and-how-video-games-are-addressing-history

know the main character at an intensely intimate and personal level without ever seeing her over 21 years of her life and eight different moves."[8]

The game is a clever way to tell the story of a character, revealing her history through the gameplay of "unpacking" her moving boxes. Through her objects, her unique living settings, and the objects owned by her housemates or partner, players are essentially peeling back a new story layer of a woman's life with each move. You get the chance to explore the space by unpacking and organizing her room. It's *Tetris* with a story. Playing the game unpacked emotions in my own life as I remembered the many moves I have made and the different people who lived (and no longer live) with me. The best storytelling in games makes you reflect on your own life.

Playing games is also one of the best ways to explore new worlds anonymously in a safe setting. When I first played *Journey* (2012), I was challenged to think differently about how I perceived the world. The impatient, productive, efficient part of me kept asking: "What's the point of all this? Where am I going? What am I supposed to do? What's my mission?"

The game was developed by Thatgamecompany, whose website describes it as "Soar above ruins and glide across sands as you explore the secrets of a forgotten civilization."[9] The "point" of the game is to simply explore. And what a beautiful world and landscape the game makers designed. It's calm, mysterious, and curious, all at the same time. The entire game feels like a metaphor for life. We don't know why we're here, but while we're here, we can enjoy the time, explore, and connect with people we meet along the way. The point is there is no other point. Perhaps the point is to be present.

As a participant, I'd like to experience more places where I can simply wander and not *have* to do anything. Places like Meow Wolf, an immersive art experience started in 2008 by a group of artists in

---

[8] https://peabodyawards.com/award-profile/unpacking/
[9] https://thatgamecompany.com/journey/

Santa Fe, New Mexico, offer these types of immersive worlds where you can simply explore and discover places of surprise and delight. The creators now have set up five different locations in the United States, all with unique stories and themes, but that live in the same "multiverse." In the original location, House of Eternal Return, visitors can walk up to a seemingly normal house but find themselves climbing into a washing machine, which takes you down a slide to a different space. Or walking into a fridge to find themselves in a mirrored hallway. Or crawling into a fireplace and discovering a magical cave where you can play music on a mastodon's bones. It's hard to describe what the space is unless you've experienced it. The guest promise is surprise and delight in an unexpected adventure. Therefore, visitors should come with a curious and playful mindset. Perhaps the emotional takeaway is that we should never stop exploring. We should always go to unfamiliar places so that we may discover more of ourselves.

EMOTIONAL

Some of the best games make me feel a range of different emotions. There are people who say playing games and "fake" worlds like theme parks and immersive experiences aren't "real." Of course they are. Reality is simply a matter of perspective. What's real to one person may not be real to someone else. The only way you can tell if something is real is if you *feel* something. You can't deny your emotions; they're absolutely real. When a game or experience makes you feel a certain emotion, for that moment in time, you are as real and human as you'll ever be. You're so present in the moment that you don't think of anything else. You simply feel, which is something that we all crave in our ordinary lives: to feel something, anything at all. And to feel it with the people who you're with, to connect and engage with them, and to connect with strangers around you. There's no better feeling than having a shared experience together.

Gaming also helps me become a more empathetic human being because I get to look at the world through the lens of another person. In games, I've played every gender, race, nationality, age, and profession. I empathize with the character, their story, and the situation. I root for them because I'm rooting for myself. What better way to connect with our own humanity than through the lives of others? Gaming is such a powerful way for us to understand and empathize with others unlike us. We empathize through the emotions that we experience in the game. By walking in someone else's shoes, we get a first-person perspective of what that experience feels like.

In the realm of immersive experiences, *The Nest* by Scout Expedition Co. is an immersive, dramatic, and emotional "intimate live experience combining elements of immersive theater, video games, and escape rooms. Equipped with only a flashlight and cassette deck, you'll explore the winding corridors of a storage unit once owned by a woman named Josie. By examining her personal effects and listening to the audio diary she left behind, you'll slowly piece together the surreal, heartbreaking, and beautiful narrative of Josie's life . . . and in so doing, come to realize just how precious

The Nest. Photo by Jeremey Connors courtesy of Scout Expedition Co.

memories are."[10] This is such a moving and intimate experience that you'll want to share it with others once you've experienced it.

Escape room experiences are some of the most powerful emotional experiences I've been in. Besides the feeling of urgency, fear, and panic, I also feel a sense of teamwork and camaraderie with the people I'm with. We're stuck together in a space, challenged to communicate and work together so that we can solve a problem.

In our modern society, there aren't many instances in our lives (thankfully) where we have to work together as a family or group of friends in a "life or death" situation. Escape rooms are a great way to experience that without the real consequence of danger or death. Some escape rooms are more effective than others, but when they're done right, they can be so emotionally powerful. We feel scared together. We are challenged together, and we help each other get "to the other side" physically and psychologically.

How do you know when your experience is emotional? Trust your instincts. Your own instincts as well as others'. Personally, I know that my experience is emotional when I literally get goose bumps. Bring trusted friends and colleagues to experience it and playtest with them.

EVERGREEN

Finally, the best games are timeless. Every generation can appreciate the game. It's classic and evergreen. There are very few games that can hold this designation. They are the tried-and-true games that will speak to generations for many years to come. They include the *Tomb Raider* and *Super Mario* franchises, the *Zelda* games, and, for many, *Call of Duty*.

No one has the perfect formula for creating a timeless game. It's for the player to ultimately decide whether it's a game worth playing again or not. The same goes for immersive places. It's the

---

[10] https://www.hatchescapes.com/the-nest

participant who decides that a place like Disneyland is worth going to again and again, until it's not. How long can a place hold such a designation? Only time will tell.

What makes an experience evergreen is elusive. If someone knew the formula to make evergreen experiences, then they would have no competition. I think, in this industry, competition is good. We should be upping our game every time we create something new. We want to become the next great thing, place, or experience. Creating something evergreen involves understanding your participant or user intimately and authentically. The attempt forces you as the creator to look outside of yourself and consider the people who are actually going through your experience. Only by designing the experience with the participant in mind can you create something truly evergreen.

With that said, here are some considerations that will help you make your experience evergreen, regardless of whether you're designing a theme park, a museum, an art installation, a VR experience, or an indoor playground.

Universal Themes

Focus on themes and concepts that are not bound by current trends or fads. Choose universal and timeless topics that resonate with a broad, global audience of varying ages and carry enduring significance. Themes like love, nature, adventure, exploration, wonder, magic, and mystery. Focus on the core aspects of the human condition that can transcend time and remain relatable for all types of participants.

This is what Joe Rohde and his team did with Pandora – The World of Avatar. By creating a fictional land that was aligned with Animal Kingdom's three core values (Intrinsic Value of Nature, Transformation through Adventure, and Personal Call to Action), he and his team maintained a creative integrity and consistency that resonated throughout the land. The story of the land was rooted in a universal theme: the human relationship with nature.

Depth and Complexity

Create layers of depth and complexity within your immersive experience to offer something more than meets the eye in the first visit. This allows participants to discover new details and meanings upon repeated interactions and visits, ensuring that the experience remains engaging and thought-provoking. Consider how you can plug in more content and programming throughout the year based on the fluctuating levels of audience engagement.

In my first book, *Immersive Storytelling for Real and Imagined Worlds*, I discuss the importance of understanding the different kinds of museum visitors: the streakers, strollers, and students (terms coined in the 1990s by George MacDonald, an anthropologist and museum administrator). Another common analogy refers to the waders, swimmers, and divers. There are participants who prefer to engage with the surface-level story (the streakers) and hit the highlights. There are those who want to learn a little bit more about each element (the strollers), and finally, there are the students or scholars, who want to know and do EVERYTHING within the experience.

Who are the Spectator, the Casual Gamer, and the Completionist?

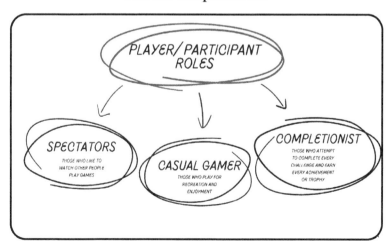

In gaming terms, there are many different types of players, but for our purposes, let's simplify it down to three participant roles relevant to immersive experiences, similar to the museum analogy: the streakers are the spectators (those who like to watch other people play games), the strollers are the casual gamers (those who play for recreation and enjoyment), and the scholars are the completionists (those who attempt to complete every challenge and earn every achievement or trophy). Completionists want to peel back every layer available in the story.

Consider all three different types of players when you design your immersive experience. The primary role of a museum is to inform, enlighten, and educate. The role of an immersive experience is to immerse, engage, and entertain. As you design your experience, ask yourself: Does every step of the journey fully engage the spectator, the casual gamer, *and* the completionist? Is there something for each one of them to do at every point of my experience? Have I given them enough choices to satisfy their desired levels of engagement? Designing for all three types offers a level of depth that can be sensed by participants no matter which type they are.

Interactivity and Choice

Gaming is all about interactivity and choice. Consider how you can incorporate elements of interactivity and choice that allow participants, whether they're a spectator, casual gamer, or completionist, to shape their experience. This increases replayability, as different choices can lead to varied outcomes. Consider your favorite video games and physical experiences (e.g., a hiking trail or playground) and how often you come back to them. There's a replayability that never gets old.

I often wonder how the use of AI (artificial intelligence) can encourage participants to come to immersive experiences and offer more choices and interactivity. Could there be a system in place that recognizes your visitor and what they did in previous visits, recalling memories, making recommendations, and engaging in dialogue with them to enhance their next experience? Can the experience become personalized and adaptable based on their previous actions? Can they meet different characters and unlock new story pathways based on what they completed previously? Can AI introduce your visitors to other visitors based on shared interests, preferences, and even proximity?

In regard to the next chapter of educational institutions, museums, and cultural institutions, can AI build an infrastructure to create a new place for learning? Imagine a place that knows the best way a child learns, remembers their progress and preferences, and encourages new pathways through the institution based on their previous visits. No longer do children (and adults) have to maintain the same learning pace as the entire class. They can learn at their own pace, in their own preferred way. Consider how visitors might unlock new levels or lessons based on their learned skills. Imagine how they can use those newly learned skills and apply them to interactive programming embedded throughout the experience.

I look forward to the day when I can engage in a place that has a collective memory of all my experiences. That perhaps can anticipate my needs and curate an experience based on my mood, past experiences, and wish fulfillment. That can make suggestions and recommendations based on my previous likes and dislikes. That actively learns and evolves to personalize my experience with each visit. That can suggest activities based on who I'm with or when I'm alone.

Flexibility and Seasonality

Design your experience with a flexible structure that allows for easy updates, expansions, or additions. This enables you to introduce new content or new features to keep the content fresh. Plan a schedule for regular updates, events, or challenges within the immersive experience. This encourages participants to revisit the experience and engage with the new content.

This is obviously easier said than done, but as designers, we have to be mindful of creating our experiences with flexibility to adapt to updated information, emerging technologies, and new platforms. Consider how to future-proof your immersive experience so that it can be imported to new devices or environments. Can your experience be easily movable and adaptable to other locations? Can the experience come to the participants rather than the other way around?

Introduce seasonality to your experience so visitors can have a different overlay depending on the changing themes of the seasons. *Fortnite Battle Royale* accomplishes this very effectively with their seasons, each lasting for about ten weeks. Each season introduces a new theme, along with a new chapter in the game's storyline, bringing in fresh content, exclusive skins, and updated gameplay elements.

Like *Fortnite*, your exhibits can be refreshed regularly to keep visitors coming back. This could involve rotating exhibits, adding interactive elements, or incorporating new technologies to enhance the visitor experience. Many museums adopt themed seasons or events to create excitement by celebrating what's relevant and "top of mind" for their visitors.

Fortnite also fosters a strong sense of community among its players through social features and events. As creators of immersive experiences, you can leverage social media and online platforms to build communities around your exhibits, encouraging visitors to share their experiences and engage with each other both online and offline. Depending on the size of your community, consider hiring community managers to build, grow, and manage these communities around a particular brand, product, or organization. They can help to engage your participants, gather feedback, serve as a bridge between your organization and the community, and curate the best content.

Can you also reward visitors with in-location items and achievements for participating in seasonal events? Your immersive experience can offer incentives such as exclusive merchandise, discounts on future visits, and special access to behind-the-scenes tours to encourage repeat visits and engagement.

Ultimately, when you design your experience, consider its lifespan. If you're looking to build a place for the long haul, consider how you can be more agile in responding to changing trends, audience preferences, and current events, allowing your experience to stay relevant and attract diverse audiences.

User-Generated Content

There are plenty of games that embrace the player's inner creator. *Minecraft* allows players to build and create virtually anything they can imagine using blocks in a 3D, procedurally generated world. From towering castles to intricate contraptions, the only limit is one's imagination. *LittleBigPlanet* is a game that encourages

teamLab Planets, Tokyo, Japan. Photo by Foster Kerrison.

players to create their own levels and share them with the community. With a wide array of customization options and tools, players can design unique levels, characters, and objects, creating a vibrant and collaborative creative community.

Embrace your visitor's ability to cocreate in the context of your world. teamLab does this beautifully with their experiences, in which visitors can draw their own marine creature and upload it into the gigantic digital aquarium to see it swimming with other people's creations. They do a similar exhibit with a sky scene so visitors can draw birds and planes. When you integrate a mechanism that allows participants to contribute their own content or stories to the experience, they feel more engaged creatively.

I mentioned AI in the section on visitor interactivity and choice. Consider how AI can assist in building user-generated content that visitors have created at home, online, or on-site to play and engage with in your experience. Could they create their own avatar that can join them in their adventure? Could they create or earn rewards and objects that they can then utilize in the physical experience? Could they create their own world in the context of your sandbox? Could they engage in your experience by selecting their preferred mode of difficulty, ranging from newbie to pro? Imagine going through some of your favorite interactive attractions with the ability to set the difficulty level. Visitors would most certainly return to that attraction many more times.

Cross-Media Integration

Extend the immersive experience to multiple media platforms, such as pop-up events, books, films, games, and social media. This cross-media integration can create a broader universe for participants to explore and engage with. You may be surprised how you can attract different audiences with one medium and not the other. Explore your options and create opportunities for future fans to engage with your content in different ways.

Walt Disney was the original visionary when it comes to cross-media integration. He had the foresight to merchandise his shows, movies, and, eventually, theme parks. He created a TV show to market his work and found new mediums for sharing his stories and creating engagement with his fans, from books to movies to live events.

Netflix is also doing exciting work in cross-media integration. Let's not forget that they used to be a DVD rental service. Today, they're a content juggernaut, a force to be reckoned with in the storytelling space. From streaming TV series and movies on the screen to offering online video games and real-life experiential events, they are continually broadening their audiences and giving them the opportunity to engage with their content in new and unique ways. They're playing the attention and engagement game like no other company is doing right now. I admire their ability to move fast and ride on the popularity wave of their content.

Community Engagement

Community is everything in the gaming world. These communities provide opportunities for social interaction and connection. Players can engage with others who share similar interests, form friendships, and collaborate on in-game activities. This social aspect enhances the gaming experience and can contribute to a sense of belonging and camaraderie.

Create a strong sense of belonging and a feeling of community in your immersive experience. By fostering a strong community, you encourage your participants to share their thoughts, experiences, and interpretations. Consider how you can continually cultivate an ongoing dialogue that adds depth to the overall experience. Create a home base for your fans: a place where like-minded people can find one another. Are there fan groups that you can support and engage with from around the world? Are there opportunities for members to meet online?

Feedback and Iteration

Last but not least, pay attention to participant feedback and use it to iteratively improve and enhance the experience. The gaming world constantly updates their content based on player feedback. We can learn from this open feedback loop. This ensures that you're addressing any issues and continuously refining the content. Hold regular focus groups and feedback sessions throughout the year. Survey visitors and ask for their honest response to your experience. Be open and listen. Most importantly, be willing to evolve and change, or the world will pass you by.

In summary, we're reminded that the essence of great storytelling in gaming lies not just in entertaining players, but in immersing them in worlds that educate, engage, and evoke emotions. By embracing the 6 Es — engaging, educational, emotional, experimental, exploratory, and evergreen — game developers have the power to craft experiences that transcend the confines of entertainment, leaving a lasting impact on players' lives. The lessons learned from the 6 Es guide us toward the creation of experiences that captivate, inspire, and endure for generations to come.

JUMP-STARTER QUESTIONS

- Have you captured the 6 Es of Great Storytelling in Games? Is your experience engaging, educational, emotional, experimental, exploratory, and evergreen?
- When will you playtest your experience with an audience, receive their feedback, and reiterate? Plan for it.

CUTSCENE: AN INTERVIEW WITH TODD MARTENS[11]

|||||||||||||||||||||||||||||||||||||||||||||||||||||||||||||||||||||||||||||||||||||

Interactive entertainment and theme park journalist
for the *Los Angeles Times*

MK: What are some of your favorite theme parks, games, and immersive places? What makes you come back to them again and again?

TM: Art museums and Disneyland. In some ways, you would think that they're on opposite ends of the spectrum. You would think that Disneyland is this place to go with family, friends, and it's a place to go to experience lightheartedness and be playful and silly. And then a museum is a place you go to enrich yourself and learn. But I think they're actually connected. They're both about making sense of our lives through storytelling. You get a sense of what came before, and where we are and who we are. I think both of them are vital. I don't necessarily think of a place like Disneyland as an escape. I think we go there to make sense of the world around us.

MK: What are some of the things that you hope to see more of in art museums and in theme parks?

TM: Over the last five to ten years, the emphases we've seen are on "immersive spaces." The theme park industry has done this for decades, but I think I really see cultural institutions looking toward the theme park industry and toward creating a theme space.

When I go to a museum, I want a sense of the story that is being told. If you go to the Huntington, you can see a wide cross section of really elegant pieces and housewares, and sometimes that art is confounding as to why it might be there.

---

[11] This interview was conducted by Margaret Kerrison over video chat and email. The transcript has been edited for clarity and length.

You need a greater sense of time and place, and a greater sense of how something was viewed in the time period it was viewed. So you don't feel like you're just walking into a building with white walls. Like the place is the art, and a little bit more of how that art was meant to be seen. It's embracing the theater of it, embracing the theatricality of why we go to these spaces.

We're so wedded to our devices and our our phones and our laptops and computers. When we go to these spaces, what we're really looking for is a little bit of a sense of awe and wonder. Anything that inspires that curiosity. Anything that draws you to it.

MK: What spaces have evoked a sense of awe and wonder for you recently?

TM: Astra Lumina in Orange County. What struck me with Astra Lumina is that it went beyond something that is beautiful to look at. And it was beautiful to look at, but it also had a narrative. It had those multiple layers that I'm looking for. You could go there and you could take a photo with your friends, and it could be a very lovely moment, or you could sort of read the plaques and embrace the mystical ambient audio and go deeper into this narrative about what would happen if the stars came to Earth. It does have some nods for science and to astronomy theory, but it doesn't get too heavy on that. It gives you a space to wander and wonder, and it gives you a space to construct a narrative. It drew me to it because it reminded me on a much smaller, local scale of what Meow Wolf is doing across the country in their spaces, putting local regional artists together by giving it narrative, giving it a sense of play.

If you want to go deeper, you can. If you just want to go and have a nice night out by yourself or with your friends, you can also do that. But I thought Astra Lumina did a really good job, especially in a major city like Los Angeles, where stargazing can be difficult, creating that sense of beauty we can get from being out in nature and realizing that we are part of something much bigger.

MK: What do you think we are missing as a community? What do you long for when you go places?

TM: Coming from somebody who grew up with games, and somebody who writes about games, I'm really looking for a sense of play. When you think of the pandemic, how games were created, there was a sense of community; whether that was through *Among Us* or *Animal Crossing*, people were playing online. I think a lot of the stories and a lot of the narrative of that was when we couldn't go out and socialize, this gave us a way to socialize.

But the real lesson is — I think, so often in our adult lives, we move away from a sense of playfulness, using play to bring us together. My last relationship, we probably had the best first date because we went to the Arboretum. But instead of just walking around the Arboretum, we used the setting of the Arboretum and our mobile phones to play a game of hide-and-go-seek. And I think that accelerated how quickly we got to know each other. Because when you're communicating in a playful setting in the safeness of rules, you let yourself ease into a place a little bit more. So I'm not saying every place needs to be filled with games, but I think cultural institutions could do a better job of not necessarily always being so self-serious. It can be a game as simple as asking patrons of an art museum what painting they would want in their home and why. To get us to think about these sorts of questions and engage with art on a personal level.

MK: What would you like to see more (or less) of in designed places and experiences?

TM: I'm not the biggest fan of this trend of immersive art projection on a wall. I feel like those lack the edification, the knowledge base that I'm bringing home with me. I also think being conscious of allowing you to navigate the exhibits in a way that creates a sense of exploration, in a way that creates a sense of how this object may have been displayed as opposed to something that's just placed in a container, or behind a ribbon. You don't want to feel like you're just moving through rooms. You want to feel like you're moving through a space.

I think we're at an interesting point in history where a lot of our design spaces are driven by commerce. Here in Los Angeles and around the country, you see shopping centers that are designed to look like old-fashioned main streets. What I really want to see are places that are designed around community and encourage a sense of playfulness. Not just nostalgia but a sense of playfulness and a sense of curiosity. But I think overall, a space that is welcoming. A space that encourages you to look up at it, and encourages you to walk around, walk in, and walk under. Places that encourage wandering in a sense of curiosity.

MK: How do you think immersive storytellers of physical places and experiences can learn from video game techniques?
TM: This is interesting because I've long believed that one of the most influential texts on video games is Disneyland's original Pirates of the Caribbean. In many ways, it's akin to modern open-world video games, though it is created in a physical space and includes no specific interactive points. The interactivity is all in our minds. It is our choice, for instance, which storylines to follow, what pirates to listen to, and what tales to concoct out of the facial expressions and limited body movements. The storyline of the attraction — like the best theme park rides — is a little abstract. It's not a linear plot, as the attraction jumps through time, flirts with mysticism, and allows us to draw our own conclusions about what it all means. It's a theme park ride that evokes wonder and offers us our own paths to dial into. I've thought of Pirates of the Caribbean often as I've played many a modern video game.

Pivotal interactive works like *The Legend of Zelda: Tears of the Kingdom* feature a like-minded approach to nonlinear storytelling; it's up to us, for instance, what puzzles to solve, what characters to get to know, and what plot threads to follow. One is a physical creation in a theme park, and one is a digital, malleable world, but both allow us the opportunity for discovery and the illusion of defining our own narrative.

I think that's the original lesson — and the core lesson. Video games and technology advance rapidly, and it's easy to be seduced by wanting to work with what's new and what's experimental. That's one of the joys of working in immersive spaces, but I really think the best games are the ones that focus on playfulness and curiosity. It's more about creating a space to ask questions than it is to solve quests.

When I think of the best times I've had in immersive spaces, they've been ones that allowed me to simply play — a loved one giving me a light and unexpected push out of nowhere in *Star Wars*: Galaxy's Edge, saying to me, "What's a respectable guy like you doing hanging with a scoundrel like me?" Or even times on my own in Pandora – The World of Avatar, trying to create my own storylines out of the scenery. What kind of creature is that? Who constructed this bridge? New Orleans Square, the Wizarding World of Harry Potter, and, of course, Super Nintendo World are places to simply play. Super Nintendo World does something quite genius but very simple — the official gamelike trappings are built into the surroundings as if they belong there. We're asked to touch and experiment with the environment. We wander and explore as we would through a national park. It's not about bringing a video game into our own world but simply remembering that our world is one that naturally invites play.

There are all sorts of topics and subtopics that allow for more complex conversations, especially when considering alternate reality games, immersive theater, or escape rooms. And making puzzles diegetic — remembering that humans don't speak in code — is a game design challenge that continues to evolve. These are worthy and deserving of deep analysis, but it all falls apart if the focus strays too far from human curiosity. Whether it's *Sleep No More* or the late great Adventurers Club at Walt Disney World's Pleasure Island, these experiences work because they meet us where we're at, invite us in, and don't demand we play a specific role. The role remains up to us. Everyone in the immersive space has no doubt heard the anecdote of Walt Disney referring to Pirates of the Caribbean as an attraction that's akin to being at a cocktail party, where we hear snippets of conversations and come back to hear more. That's play. We're choosing our own paths to follow. A good, effective game can be as simple as placing a sword in a stone and inviting guests to try to remove it. For that brief moment, we're whatever character we want to be.

"Now that I've worked on a few games, I've grappled with the degree to which games are not really a writer's medium. Film's not really a writer's medium, either. Good writing certainly doesn't hurt, but it's not the thing that saves the day. . . . Games are primarily about a connection between the player, the game world, and the central mechanic of the game. They're about creating a space for the player to engage with that mechanic and have the world react in a way that feels interesting and absorbing but also creates a sense of agency."

— Tom Bissell, journalist, critic, and writer

4

WRITING THROUGH THE PLAYER'S PERSPECTIVE

W HAT DOES WRITING through the player's perspective mean? It simply means that when you imagine an experience, you write for the *player's* experience. You are designing for your end user and not for yourself.

This may seem obvious, but it's not regularly practiced. As creators and designers, we tend to design for ourselves and for each other, but not for our users or participants. We often feel clever about the things we design and pat each other on the backs for our beautiful work.

Instead, as narrative champions, we should advocate for the participant experience first and foremost, which means looking at the experience through *their* perspective, and not ours. If we create experiences in a vacuum of like-minded people who want to create to delight in our own designs, we have failed as designers. The participant perspective and experience should always come first. In fact, the intention of our design should stem from the participant's wish fulfillment. It should ask the all-important question:

How do you want your participants to feel?

With a mindset focused on wish fulfillment, you can then consider how the participant might become the hero of their own journey. In their best forms, the gaming and themed entertainment or immersive storytelling industries share many similarities because they aim to give the participant the agency to influence their own story within the context of the imagined world.

Immersive storytelling describes creating a space using different kinds of technology to build a sense of presence for the participant. The space can be a combination of physical, digital, and virtual elements, and ultimately, it gives the participant a transportive feeling within an emotionally compelling story as if they are "really there." It's designed to be so compelling that it makes participants feel like they're part of that world and, hopefully, makes them believe that they belong in it and can influence it. It's an impactful technique that captures the emotion and wish fulfillment of that experience.

This shouldn't be new to you. But if you reread the previous paragraph, you'll notice what immersive storytelling isn't: a list of instruction in which you tell participants what to do, or a story about some *other* characters with no connection to the participants.

In my second book, *Reimagined Worlds*, I emphasize the importance of defining the guest's wish fulfillment in one phrase:

Form and Function follow Fulfillment.

I argue that defining the form and the function are secondary to understanding what will lead to fulfillment for the guest. In other terms, the place and the purpose are less important than defining the promise (the wish fulfillment of every visitor, user, or participant) of your experience.

Immersive storytelling can also be referred to as experience design, themed experience, immersive experience, and, in its most extreme form, world building. The story can take place in many physical and digital environments: a theme park, museum, house, small exhibit, corporate center, restaurant, store, online learning site, VR experience, game, and more.

When I first started working at Walt Disney Imagineering, one of the first things we learned was to "walk in our guest's shoes," meaning we needed to take a step back from being the "creator" and experience the theme park through the visitor's point of view. This is what Walt Disney encouraged all of his Imagineers to do. Imagineers don't receive any special privileges to jump the queues in the parks. We have to wait in line, experience the crowds and the heat, and appreciate what our guests have to go through with every visit. We go through the experience, world, and story through their lens. Does it feel immersive and engaging? Does it make sense? Is it a fun journey for all ages? Is it inclusive and welcoming to all guests? Even before the experience opens, we are the ones to "test" the experience to make sure that it is the most engaging and immersive that it can be. We are the pre-guest, or what some people refer to as "guest zero."

When gamers first play a game, they are introduced to a whole new world with an unfamiliar set of rules and characters. They must understand what's going on, what they have to do, who they have to meet, and where they need to go. They should also understand *why* they are going on their journey. As I mentioned earlier, guests in a theme park take on a similar role in that they go through a world as the hero of their own journey. They should be encouraged to explore and discover new people and places that will send them down different paths.

WRITING THE GUEST JOURNEY

Writing from a first-person perspective can be used in multiple guest experiences, not just theme park or gaming-centric attractions. It's good practice to write your guest experience from a first-person perspective so you can walk in your visitor's shoes, scene by scene.

Whether you're designing a theme park ride, retail experience, or any other kind of world, a creator should always consider how their visitor will experience it holistically. As in gaming, you must consider the player first. The player experience in gaming storytelling is a multifaceted journey, guided by the combination of narrative, gameplay, and immersion. At its core lies the player's ability to inhabit and shape the world presented to them, becoming the hero of their own story. From the moment they embark on their adventure, players are drawn into a rich tapestry of characters, conflicts, and quests, each carefully crafted to captivate their imagination and evoke emotion. As they navigate through the game world, players are not mere spectators, but active participants in the unfolding narrative, making choices that influence the course of events and shape their character's destiny. Whether they're exploring vast open worlds, solving intricate puzzles, or engaging in intense battles, every interaction contributes to the player's sense of agency and immersion, deepening their connection to the story and its inhabitants. Storytelling in games is a deeply personal and transformative journey, in which players often uncover the power of their own imagination.

In theme parks, we are already accustomed to gaming storytelling techniques in attractions such as Buzz Lightyear Astro Blasters and Toy Story Midway Mania! More recently, there are attractions like LEGO NINJAGO The Ride, Mario Kart: Bowser's Challenge, and WEB SLINGERS: A Spider-Man Adventure, all interactive rides using 3D glasses and gesture-recognition technology through which guests can influence their actions, but all within the confines of the predetermined story. This type of ride immerses guests in the world, and in the gameplay and actions of the world, with some feeling of agency. However, many argue that the gameplay itself deters from the story rather than making sense within the story. Although these are very fun rides, especially for young kids, they don't necessarily communicate the meaning of the story well enough for us to be engaged in the story itself.

Adopting a first-person perspective in writing doesn't automatically guarantee an engaging experience. It's important that this choice hold significance within the framework of the narrative and the universe you're constructing. The mere use of the first-person viewpoint doesn't serve as an answer for all challenges you might encounter. You have to prioritize the WHY of your experience so that it drives your participants' actions to make sense in the greater scheme of the narrative. These actions must seamlessly harmonize with the overarching themes, narrative, and setting.

So how can you successfully use storytelling techniques in gaming to create a believable, emotionally engaging immersive experience?

Instead of passively observing a story, the participant is given choices at various points in the narrative. These choices can affect the direction of the story, leading to different outcomes and branching storylines. It offers the participant a sense of agency and involvement in shaping the story's progression. Just like in games, gamified stories offer feedback on the participant's actions and decisions. Depending on the choices made, the story may respond with different consequences, reinforcing the idea that their decisions matter.

The two-night adventure *Star Wars*: Galactic Starcruiser is an example of an interactive experience giving the participant different choices at multiple points throughout the multiday voyage. Participants could also change their minds and switch allegiances if they felt bonded to certain characters over others. Depending on who they decided to ally with, their story resulted in different actions and consequences. The overall story arc of the experience, however, remained the same. The individual choices combined with randomized assignment of activities depending on availability determined the participant's actions throughout the voyage.

In the Wizarding World of Harry Potter, eager participants wait their turns at several locations to wield their infrared remote-control wands and attempt the art of spell casting. After finding these locations, positioned thoughtfully throughout various corners of this land, a participant can initiate uncomplicated interactive movements upon themed prop sets arranged behind storefront window displays, resulting in an engaging gameplay experience.

Participants feel a sense of accomplishment even though there are no physical or virtual rewards. They are driven by the reward that they have agency to "cause something to happen" in the

The Wizarding World of Harry Potter, Universal Studios Hollywood.
Photo by Margaret Kerrison.

environment. It's a modern evolution of the "shooting gallery" and other boardwalk games.

Ultimately, it's good practice to try writing from your guest's perspective so you can walk in your participant's footsteps, scene by scene, interaction by interaction, action by action. Does the action match the narrative and support the context of the world? Does it make sense? Is there a good reason why participants are doing what they're doing? Does anything need to be tweaked or changed so that the participant isn't just "doing something cool" without much intention behind it?

There have been many times in my career when a team has designed an innovative ride system or wanted to implement a new technology at their site without a clearly defined story. They often bring in a writer or storyteller at the last minute to help identify the narrative and guest journey, when they should have included the storyteller from the very beginning of the process.

Writers or storytellers are integral in identifying and defining the overarching narrative or thematic structure that encompasses and guides the entire experience. In the context of a theme park ride, the narrative manifests in all of the related spaces, from the moment your visitors queue for a ride to the moment they exit the attraction. Why is creating a cohesive narrative framework important? Because it helps build a sense of continuity and immersion, allowing visitors to feel like they're part of a larger narrative as they progress through different stages of the ride. It gives context and meaning. It prevents the participant from being "pulled out" of the story because they're confused, uninterested, or frustrated.

OUR OWN WORLD AS IMMERSIVE SPACE

I'm often inspired by the most random and seemingly mundane things and places. As a creative, I think in metaphors and connect dots between things that seemingly don't make sense at first, yet they make sense from a feeling, qualitative point of view. I write down what I feel so that I can make sense of it as I write about it.

I recently taught a seminar called Immersive Storytelling and Narrative Placemaking in Architecture at Cal Poly Pomona's School of Architecture. Oftentimes, writers, creators, architects, and designers create from their own perspective and not the visitors'. We need to shift that mindset in all spaces so we can consider the user or participant first and foremost.

In this course, I took my students to visit places like the Huntington Library, Art Museum, and Botanical Gardens in San Marino, California, and the Getty Center in Los Angeles to observe their surroundings, take photos, and describe their guest flow and journey through a written first-person perspective. They had to write and document their experience as a visitor so they could understand what it FEELS like to walk in the visitor's shoes. What is their experience like from beginning to end? What do they see, do, hear, feel, taste, and touch as they go through their journey?

The Huntington Library, Art Museum, and Botanical Gardens, San Marino, CA.
Photo by Margaret Kerrison.

What can be modified to ensure their comfort and safety? What needs to change to immerse them in a more compelling and engaging story?

As in games, physical spaces incorporate a sense of reward, cost, duration, and maybe even competition, as well as a promise and parameters or rules within the world. Are your visitors asked to play a specific role when entering the space? What agency are you offered as a participant? Do you have an agenda, mission, or purpose? Do you have a set amount of time to fulfill your promise?

This is the exercise that I posed to my students, and I encourage you to try it the next time you go through an experience:

> *Based on your site visit, write approximately 1,500 words summarizing the guest experience from your POV. Add photo documentation (approximately 5–10 images). Describe your visitor flow and what you see, do, feel, and observe. Describe the setting: the mood, lighting, textures,*

*colors, objects, and overall environment. What worked,
what didn't? What was your feeling before you entered the
site, during the visit, and after? What did you learn? Were
you the target audience? If yes, why? If no, who is the target audience? Did you gain any new insights to the place or
subject matter? Were you changed? If so, how? Would you
return? If so, would you experience the site differently? If
so, why and how?*

Keep a journal as you go through experiences. Jot down your
thoughts, insights, and impressions. It's good practice in writing
from a first-person perspective. These days, I always keep a little
notebook with me wherever I go, because you never know when
inspiration will strike you.

Your guest journey should tell a story. It should focus on the
feelings and actions of the participant. Every step of the way, the
participant's basic needs must be met, physically and psychologically. We move through the scenes and the rooms like we're
navigating a world in a game.

Whether you're designing a theme park ride, retail experience, or any other kind of built environment, a creator should
always consider how their guest or participant will experience it
holistically.

JUMP-STARTER QUESTIONS

- How will you give agency to your participant? What is the
  gameplay of your experience? At what points will you give
  them choices to make?
- How will you immerse the participant in all of their
  senses?
- What is the guest flow? How will they physically experience your story?

"You can't stay in your corner of the Forest waiting for others to come to you. You have to go to them sometimes."

— Winnie the Pooh

5

LEVEL-SET: MEET YOUR PARTICIPANTS WHERE THEY ARE

|||||||||||||||||||||||||||||||||||||||||||||||||||||||||||||||||||||||||||||||||||||||||||||||||||||||||||||||||||||||||||||||||||||||||||||||||||||||||

MAGINE YOUR PARTICIPANT coming to your experience. They are coming from their familiar lives, ready to embark on an adventure into an unfamiliar world. In designing your experience, you must prepare your participant for what's to come. You have to "level-set" and make sure that they're on the same page.

In other words, you're bringing everyone up to speed so no one feels lost or confused or has a sense that they don't belong. This is a social agreement that everyone abides by when they enter your experience — a mutual understanding of what's to come before they fully commit.

Joseph Campbell introduced a concept called "the monomyth" or "the hero's journey" that serves as a story template and common narrative archetype shared by different myths from around the world and outlines the different stages in the hero's journey. In writing for linear storytelling, one of the first stages in the character's story represents the "status quo." It's a Latin phrase which literally means the "state in which,"[12] meaning the current situation or the way things are now. The hero is in their familiar world, where things are just the way they are, but a story doesn't begin unless there's a "call to adventure," a conflict that arises, which prompts the hero to take action and "cross the threshold."

Campbell's monomyth is a great model for linear storytelling, but in creating immersive experiences in a physical world,

---

[12] https://www.dictionary.com/browse/status-quo

storytelling is experienced holistically, not necessarily linearly. This storytelling framework, however, is still useful in pointing out the significance of the participant's call to adventure.

In immersive storytelling, a call to adventure, also known as a "call to action," refers to an invitation given to the participant to take a particular action before, during, or after experiencing the story. It's a powerful tool used to engage the participant, create a sense of urgency, and encourage them to do something in response to the narrative.

A call to action is clear, concise, and aligned with the story's purpose and intended outcome. It helps drive engagement and empowers the audience to take action beyond merely consuming the story passively. It gives your participant an emotional takeaway that extends to their regular lives — a drive to do something based on the transformation they experienced from your story.

In other words:

Create a story that your participant WANTS to be a part of.

In order to emotionally move and transform your participant, you must have their undivided attention so that they are fully aware of their surroundings. Getting their attention, maintaining it without distractions, and creating intentional spatial awareness is all about noticing the details and carefully curating the guest flow (how your guests move through your experience in the context of your story).

To learn more about the hero's journey, I recommend reading Christopher Vogler's *The Writer's Journey: Mythic Structure for Writers* to delve deeper into this comprehensive theory of story structure and character development using examples from myths, fairy tales, and classic movies.

Vogler breaks down all the crucial storytelling elements of Campbell's hero's journey. In describing the dramatic function of a hero, he writes, "Stories invite us to invest part of our personal identity in the Hero for the duration of the experience. In a sense we become the Hero for a while. We project ourselves into the

Hero's psyche, and see the world through her eyes. Heroes need some admirable qualities, so that we want to be like them."[13]

This relates back to the idea of the guest promise and their wish fulfillment. Who do your participants imagine themselves to be when they enter your experience? What is the expectation of their identity and role? Who do they WANT to be?

In the context of gaming, "level-setting" your experience involves establishing a starting point for the player that aligns with their current knowledge, skills, and preferences. When players first enter a game, they may have varying levels of experience and familiarity with the game mechanics, story, and world. By level-setting, game designers provide players with a suggestion or indication of what to expect and where to begin based on their existing level of knowledge or skill.

For example, in a role-playing game (RPG), the player might be given the option to choose their character's difficulty level or starting attributes, allowing them to tailor the gameplay experience to their preferences and skill level. In a tutorial or introductory sequence, the game might provide hints, tips, or guidance to help new players acclimate to the game mechanics and controls, while more experienced players may have the option to skip or bypass these introductory segments.

By level-setting the experience, game designers make the players feel comfortable and engaged from the moment they begin playing, regardless of their prior experience with the game or genre. This approach helps to create a more inclusive and more accessible gaming experience, where players of all levels can enjoy and appreciate the game's challenges and rewards.

LEVEL-SETTING IN IMMERSIVE EXPERIENCES

In an immersive experience, you level-set by meeting your participant where they are with a suggestion or indication of what

---

[13] Vogler, *The Writer's Journey 25th Anniversary Edition*, 32.

to expect, what role they play, and where to begin based on their existing level of knowledge or skill.

Whether you're designing a museum or another kind of immersive experience, there are many ways you can level-set and get your participant's attention. One of the oldest tricks is to create a moment in which your participants move through a space that signifies "crossing the threshold." This is a literary device first introduced by Joseph Campbell in his book *The Hero with a Thousand Faces*, later further clarified by Vogler. This is the moment when the hero, your participant, leaves their ordinary world and enters the extraordinary world. It can come in the form of opening a door, walking down a hallway, entering a small room, walking through a projection-mapped tunnel, or riding in a vehicle that literally transports your visitor into the world (e.g., a monorail, a train, an elevator, an escalator). The crossing of the threshold should feel like such a sharp contrast to the ordinary world that your participants are leaving behind. They should feel like Alice in Wonderland, stepping into an exciting, unknown world that beckons to be explored.

Your participants have dedicated their time, money, and attention to your experience, so you want to make them feel engaged and rewarded. They *chose* to give their attention to your experience. They are spoiled for choice when it comes to what they should pay attention to, so don't waste it.

Another way to level-set is by creating a preshow. This is a great starter to not only welcome your visitors, but to set their expectations of what they're about to experience, give context and introduce the world and their role within it, and establish the visitor's purpose or mission.

This can be done verbally, visually, or practically, by handing out a card, prop, or something similar. Consider how your participant can come as who they are in the context of your world and story. Instead of forcing a specific character on each participant, consider what they need to play a believable role in your experience.

For example, in *Sleep No More*, each audience member receives a mask, to distinguish between performer and participant, but this simple practical gesture also adds a layer of anonymity that feels very *Eyes Wide Shut* (Stanley Kubrick's 1999 film). It emboldens the participant to explore the experience as an anonymous voyeur.

In Derek DelGaudio's show *In & Of Itself*, he immediately includes the audience member by giving them the agency to choose from a large selection of identifier cards. These preprinted cards describe who the audience member thinks they are (e.g., I am a hopeless romantic; I am a fighter pilot; I am a hobbyist; I am a nobody.). This simple act builds to a great emotional payoff at the end of the show.

In *Star Wars*: Galactic Starcruiser, every visitor was a "passenger" traveling on the starcruiser after boarding from their "home planet." They could choose which allegiance to join and which characters to follow and interact with in the context of the world.

Once you have the participant's attention, you can focus on setting their spatial awareness by paying attention to the details and immersing them in an extraordinary world that beckons them to explore and discover. You guide them in their journey, and give them a sense of safety and comfort so they can explore. When they feel safe, they are open and vulnerable to move from a mindset of "unlearning" to that of "learning." The stage is set for the hero of the story to embark on their adventure.

Immersive storytelling gives your audience members an opportunity to suspend their disbelief so they can fully enjoy the experience. If the format or medium is distracting or pulls them out of the story, you need to iterate and ensure that the technology is seamless and invisible. The technology should be in service to the narrative and not the other way around.

In your world, guests shouldn't think about the process or technology. They should be so emotionally engaged and immersed in the story and environment that they choose to be present and aware. As designers, we want our participants to be "in the moment" and in so much awe and wonder that they cognitively allow themselves to believe for a moment that they are in that imaginary world.

To ensure this believability, engage all of the senses. Consider what your experience looks, sounds, feels, smells, and perhaps tastes like. With engaged and heightened senses, your visitors are more likely to be aware of their surroundings and create positive associations and memories.

In a physically immersive space like Meow Wolf's House of Eternal Return, the experience is very similar to a game I mentioned in an earlier chapter, *Gone Home*. You can try to explore the house to solve the mystery of a missing family. It's a story exploration game adapted into the real world, where you don't meet any characters (except other visitors) and the story is told through the environment. The gameplay is about unraveling the mystery of the missing family by finding items, opening drawers, going into portals, and finding documents, journal entries, letters, and other clues in the form of animated videos. Some participants may choose not to engage with the story and simply have fun with the physical exploration of the experience, while others want to consume every single story element that the House offers.

In the House of Eternal Return, you aren't given a specific character to play. You are simply an explorer or investigator in the House, depending on your desired level of engagement. I imagine the creators were very much inspired by video games like *Gone Home*. Whether the participant is interested in simply interacting with the multisensory exhibit or deep-diving into the story, the House meets them where they are.

When designing your experience, consider the participant and where they are. Create a story that makes sense in the context that they find themselves in. In my recent visit to the Getty Center in Los Angeles, there was a *Play and Pastimes in the Middle Ages* exhibition. Even though my family didn't specifically come for this exhibition, it drew us in with its engaging activities, including a

Meow Wolf's House of Eternal Return, Santa Fe, NM. Photo by Margaret Kerrison.

The Getty Center, Los
Angeles, CA. Photos by
Margaret Kerrison.

medieval swordplay demonstration, an armor display, and a make-your-own-medieval-board-game workshop. It was a pleasant surprise to find something that my young gamer son would enjoy.

The call to action for this exhibition was simple. It invited its participants to embrace their curiosity and learn about medieval history through play: "Discover the lighter side of life in the Middle Ages through the surprising and engaging world of medieval games and leisure. The exhibition features dynamic images of play and explores the role of entertainment in the Middle Ages. Manuscript images capture the complex contests and pastimes that medieval people enjoyed, ranging from a lighthearted game of chess to the dangerous sport of jousting. Then as now, play was thoroughly woven into the fabric of society at every level."[14]

This exhibition was an effective way to draw participants into the world and story through play and characters. It was so effective that my ten-year-old son wanted to watch the swordplay demonstration twice on the same day. The Getty understood that their participants consisted of tourists, out-of-town visitors, locals, and families with young children. By using the context of their medieval art collection, they curated an exhibition focused on play and leisure, and they supported that concept with engaging shows and other programming that were fun for all ages.

This "meet them where they are" strategy applies to any experience you design in public spaces: malls, museums, hotels, parks, libraries, restaurants, retail, and even airports. Participants are coming to the destination for another reason, but they happen to find your experience along the way. Rather than requiring them to go to a different location for your experience, how can you bring your participants to a place that they would normally visit? You give your participants a reason to go, knowing that they have other things to do and places to go before and after your experience. This also guarantees that other members of their party will

---

[14] https://www.getty.edu/art/exhibitions/play/index.html

find things to do that interest them. Furthermore, you may create new fans or audience members that wouldn't normally visit your experience.

For example, in a visit to the outdoor mall Santa Monica Place, I happened to come across several groups of people wearing pink. I followed them and discovered that they were all dressed up to go into the World of Barbie experience. The experience had taken up a vacated store to create an immersive, interactive play space for fans of all ages. From recording a song in the Barbie Sound Studio to sliding down into the Barbie "pool," the experience created a space for fans to live their best Barbie life.

But we didn't need to be wearing pink to join in. The pop-up experience leaned on the promise of Barbie, which is to live this seemingly picture-perfect pink Malibu lifestyle. Stay in a Barbie home, drive her car, live her life. You could deduce that the fantasy is to live Barbie's life, have all of the things that she has, experience all the things that she experiences, and step into the pink, perfect fantasy of her world. And what an enticing world it is.

I saw all ages and all genders wearing pink to visit the immersive experience as well as go to the movie screening with friends and family. It was an invitation to play and engage in a story, world, community, and fantasy that *becomes their own*. They know they're not Barbie, but they can be inspired by her and her life to find their own version of it. I heard people greeting each other: "Hi Barbie!" "Hi Barbie!" It's a promise that's passed on, from one person to another. It's a promise of play and engagement, which encourages community and connection. It's a lifestyle choice. It's a state of mind.

How can you meet people where they are physically and psychologically to give them something unique and engaging? How can you use the location itself to help tell the story of your experience?

Meow Wolf's The Real Unreal, the company's fourth permanent exhibition, is located inside Grapevine Mills, a popular mall in Grapevine, TX. In their marketing, they leaned on the idea that "they found a whole new way to play . . . at the mall."[15] As always, Meow Wolf's approach is playful, experimental, and engaging. They never take themselves too seriously. They're meeting their participants "where they are" physically as well as psychologically, poking fun at the idea that people are coming to the mall to find things that "they never knew they needed and to come find themselves."

It's a fun strategy that piques the mallgoers' curiosity. What is this place? What does it all mean? What do you do inside? As their first location inside a mall, it's smaller than their other permanent exhibitions, but it invites participants who wouldn't normally come to their venues to discover their space and play. The idea that you can bring Meow Wolf to meet people "where they are" makes me believe that they will open up other locations in towns and cities that most tourists don't normally think of visiting. No longer do people have to save up enough money to book flights, hotels, and show and venue tickets to visit popular tourist destinations like New York City, Los Angeles, and Orlando. People are looking for more experiences and places to visit locally, without the big expense and time commitment.

Whenever I see experiences pop up in my frequently visited places, I support them because they encourage me to hit the "Pause" button in my life and "Press Start" to play. These places expand my imagination because they open a door to a new world, story, and characters that are waiting to be discovered. It makes me a better writer and storyteller when I have the opportunity to play in someone else's created world. It inspires me to tell better stories and encourages me to try different techniques and mediums. It helps me explore my creativity and come face-to-face with stories that surprise and challenge me.

We need to create more places to inspire play in everyone. A storytelling world that meets people where they are doesn't

---

[15] https://meowwolf.com/visit/grapevine

necessarily have to attract only gamers, as it can also beckon people who have forgotten or need to be reminded of the importance of play in our lives. We all started off as children who made playtime a constant occurrence in our daily lives. We need to be reminded of that. We need to be invited and encouraged to play again. To recapture that feeling of a friend or stranger coming up to you in a playground and asking, "Do you want to play with me?"

Additionally, consider the ways in which you can create a profound connection between participants and the characters they cross paths with, including NPCs (an abbreviation for "nonplayable characters," referring to characters outside players' control). How might these NPCs facilitate instances of engagement, drawing participants wholeheartedly into missions, stories, or realms that evoke a genuine sense of investment in the narrative's outcome? Creating opportunities for human interactions that motivate participants to take action is a powerful way to cultivate emotional attentiveness and heightened awareness.

As humans, we naturally want to help others, even strangers, when we know HOW we can help. By giving your participants simple tasks like "give this message to the woman in the blue dress" or "help me find my dog," you offer specific calls to action that your participants can immediately act upon.

As you build your world, make the interactions and tasks more interesting by adding context. For example, "give this message to the woman in the blue dress, but don't let her husband see you." Or "help me find my dog . . . He crawled into that dark tunnel and I can't fit in." By adding context, you're adding layers to the story, the character, and the world. You create surprising moments that are primed for an emotional experience.

Gamified stories often include game mechanics like points, levels, achievements, challenges, and rewards. These elements provide a sense of progress and accomplishment, motivating the audience to continue engaging with the story.

Millennium Falcon: Smugglers Run, Disneyland, Anaheim, CA. Photo by Ed Tang.

Millennium Falcon: Smugglers Run, the interactive ride in *Star Wars*: Galaxy's Edge, is an example of using game mechanics to tell a story. Based on how well your crew works together to pilot the Falcon, you earn points and explore new stages and scenes depending on your team's achievement. At the end of the ride, you're given an individual rating determined by your role as a pilot, gunner, or engineer. It's a super-challenging ride and I never score well, but coming out of the ride, my crew and I never fail to compare scores. It gives us motivation to try to do better with every ride.

Some gamified stories may include mini-games or puzzles that the audience must solve to progress in the narrative. These elements add an interactive layer to the storytelling. Users often receive rewards or recognition for completing certain tasks, making progress, or reaching specific milestones within the story. These can include virtual badges, achievements, or other forms of either in-story or real-world rewards. This is especially useful for participants who like to "collect" items, even virtual ones. By progressing in the experience, they can earn certain items and rewards by returning and engaging more deeply with the experience.

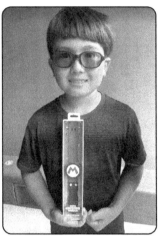

Super Nintendo World, Universal Studios Hollywood. Photos by Margaret Kerrison.

Super Nintendo World does this with their Power-Up Band. As described on their website, "Bowser Jr. has stolen the Golden Mushroom! Using your Power-Up Band, you can retrieve the Golden Mushroom for Princess Peach by playing interactive games throughout the land and collecting digital keys in order to unlock a final Shadow Showdown with Bowser Jr."[16] Of course, interactive play in theme parks is always tricky with the amount of participants engaging with them. Lines tend to form and bottlenecks are created when every participant wants to engage with the interactivity (a challenge that we'll explore in chapter 8).

All of these experiences increase the engagement of a participant throughout the story, but if an experience doesn't level-set by establishing a call to action, it won't pull them in from the very beginning. There are too many examples of immersive worlds that were built without much consideration for the participant's call to action. These fall flat because they don't answer the question of WHY participants are there, WHO they are, and WHAT they should do. I've experienced many of these places, where the space

---

[16] https://www.universalstudioshollywood.com/web/en/us/things-to-do/entertainment/key-challenges

assumes that the participants will decide what they want to do and how they want to do it. They give participants the freedom to "play" but don't level-set by assigning rules, roles, context, and *meaning* to the experience.

Your job as a designer doesn't end by simply building the playground and hoping that the participants will understand HOW to play.

This may be true of familiar settings such as playgrounds, where there are slides, swing sets, and seesaws. Children and adults know what the invitation to play is and what the social agreement is in the context of a playground. This is the beauty of teamLab's interactive installations. But in creating a metaphorical sandbox, you can't just "build it and they will come." No one will come to your experience without a strong wish fulfillment (guest promise and invitation) and call to action that are aligned within your story.

In gaming, a call to action manifests in the form of a prompt or instruction given to players to encourage them to take a particular action within the game. They serve as motivational tools to engage players, guide their progression, and ensure they have a clear sense of direction while playing. They're strategically placed not just at the beginning but throughout the game to drive player engagement and enhance the overall gaming experience.

Here are some ideas on how you can use gaming call-to-action techniques to immerse your participants:

- **Quests and Objectives:** In many RPGs, players receive quests and objectives that serve as calls to action, guiding them to explore specific areas, make allegiances, defeat certain enemies, or retrieve valuable items. They may also tactfully guide and influence players to go in another direction without being too prescriptive. Imagine how participants could receive quests and objectives in immersive experiences where they are guided and prompted to take certain actions based on their choices.

- **Tutorials:** At the beginning of a game or during new game-play mechanics, calls to action may be used to instruct players on how to perform certain actions, like movement, combat, or the use of special abilities. They encourage players to try their newly earned skills and abilities to enhance their game-play. In immersive experiences, the tutorials often emerge in the preshow, where participants learn the rules and context of the world in addition to their role and objective. Consider how tutorials can emerge as participants gain new skills and objects or complete levels in a physical experience. Could new tutorials emerge with subsequent visits?
- **Side Missions:** Games often present optional side missions or challenges, and calls to action encourage players to take on these additional tasks to earn rewards or uncover more about the game's world and story. They may be introduced to new characters and storylines that take them in another narrative direction with a different gameplay and outcome. Could side missions help to unlock certain areas that are closed to other participants? Could they uncover subplots to the larger narrative?

In a physical immersive experience, a call to action is typically at the beginning of an experience when a participant accepts the invitation to play, but they should also be peppered throughout the experience so that participants feel motivated to further engage. Participants should enter the experience with a specific, clear, concise, and consistent call to action that sets them off on their journey. They explore and interact with the story world, perhaps meeting characters along the way, just like in a video game. They may come across other calls to action to follow a different character or path (e.g., *Sleep No More*). At the end of the experience, their emotional takeaway may prompt another call to action in their regular lives. They were so moved by the experience that they see the world differently.

As an experiential designer, my objective is to ensure that all participants step out of my experience believing that they have the power to influence their own lives and contribute to making a better world.

By engaging in the sandbox, they now have the tools and the practice to influence their own lives in the real world. By assuming an identity and role with a clear objective, they FEEL important. They experience what it feels like when their actions matter, when their actions have consequences that influence the entire world. There's no greater feeling than being the hero of your own story. To feel welcomed, included, valued, and empowered.

JUMP-STARTER QUESTIONS

- What is the guest promise? What's their wish fulfillment?
- What will be your visitor's first cue that they're about to enter a new world?

CUTSCENE:
AN INTERVIEW WITH
KAMAL SINCLAIR[17]

Senior director of digital innovation at The Music Center in Los Angeles, Peabody Awards interactive board member. Former director of Sundance Institute's New Frontier Labs Program

MK: Why do you think creating digital, VR, and other physical interactive experiences is important to cultural institutions?
KS: The Music Center's Digital Innovation Initiative exists to program cultural experiences that integrate immersive, participatory, emerging, and digital technologies in new and meaningful ways for Angelenos. It also serves as a thought steward for the public to cocreate the future of culture in Los Angeles at the intersection of the arts and emerging technology.

A perpetual question in this arts sector is "What is the future of performing arts centers?" This is espccially important at a time of technological change that is creating an omni-spheric internet that is increasingly intelligent and embedded in the physicality of our cities, homes, community gathering spaces, and landscapes.

The Music Center is exploring this question through the Digital Innovation Initiative by catalyzing and supporting artists and culture makers in their experimentation with emerging technology, smart city infrastructure, community cocreation practices, and participatory art making. The Digital Innovation Initiative is working to make performing arts centers thriving players in the location-based entertainment market. We bring something that current players are not providing and emerging audiences demand — music, dance, theater, and culture that lives in blended reality. We entertain in the space between IRL and digital.

---

[17] This interview was conducted by Margaret Kerrison over email. The transcript was edited for clarity and length.

Where are we going?

Within three years, TMC Arts is known as a premier programmer of experiences that are immersive, participatory, emerging, and use creative new technology in ways that center the power of liveness and being in physical space.

Within five years, TMC is widely recognized as a trusted space for Angelenos to catalyze collective and democratized imaginations of their city's more equitable and beautiful future.

Within ten years, TMC has significantly contributed to making the arts fully integrated into every aspect of our society and resourced as an essential component of our everyday lives.

Why The Music Center? Over the last fifteen years, quality innovative cultural projects within the spectrum of physical to virtual reality have been hard to access by the public as they have primarily been presented at industry-focused film festivals, academic spaces, or artist- and technology-serving undergrounds. The more accessible or publicly engaged projects are more aligned with the visual arts than the performing arts or are tied to large-scale commercial entertainment IP (i.e., Disneyland).

The Digital Innovation Initiative wants to help fill the gaps in the field by bringing:

- innovative, high-quality, blended-reality experiences to the public at a community/city scale
- more performance-aligned productions
- more independent stories and content than large commercial offerings
- experiences created by, with, and for the public through participatory and cocreative designs
- projects with public good and community development–focused outcomes
- offerings of iconic spaces with global gravitas for the people to cultivate new cultural movements

MK: How do you balance between digital and physical in your experiences?

KS: Honestly, I have always followed the artists and the cultural makers in designing experiences from the first point of engagement with a visitor, audience member, or participant. The science and art of experience design are so nuanced and specific to each project that each one is a conversation with the makers. However, there is a core principle I stick to: It's our job to ensure the audience doesn't fail.

What I mean is interactive, participatory experiences that allow agency by the audience need to be designed so that no matter what choices they make, they are successful. We design the playground, and they play within it. Simple constraints are incredibly useful for prompting imagination and great play. Secondly, the story or the meaning making has to be the first objective. The emerging technology are just new tools for designing transformative, transcendent, fun, provocative, and meaningful experiences. Unless the technology is a machine learning AI that becomes sentient.

MK: What are the most important components of guest interactivity for you?

KS: The Music Center has a theory of change that we measure success against. It essentially breaks down to designing experiences that increase guests' physical, emotional, and mental well-being — feel their own creativity has been activated or enhanced, feel a greater sense of connection to other people involved in the experience, feel that their own experience and identity is valued, and they expand and deepen their understanding of the world and its diverse cultural, aesthetic, and artistic traditions and practices. Tall order! When vetting immersive, interactive, or participatory projects, we assess their potential to achieve one or more of these outcomes.

Additionally, we assess the project's ability to be accessible. This is part of the principle of ensuring the audience or participant doesn't fail. How are they on-ramped? How well do they understand the rules and parameters of engagement? How are they rewarded with meaningful and enriching outcomes of their actions in the experience? These are all questions we try to evaluate.

The end result of all this design strategy is not the novelty or the gadget wow factor. The purpose is to tell the story or provide an experience that can only be told or experienced in this form.

MK: What are some examples of innovative storytelling that excite you?

KS: Two projects in development that I am excited about are:

The Dream Machine by Nona Hendryx. She is collaborating with BINA48 on an immersive mixed-reality experience that provides a journey from the BINA48 Garden to an AR Bridge to a VR Dream Machine. BINA48 is the world's first Black female AI. The experience begins in her garden installation, designed by Mickalene Thomas. Audiences are immersed in conversations, art happenings, and live interactions with BINA48 herself. Next, the Bridge and AR ritual walk with music and visual art from Cyboracle (Nona), bringing the Dreamers together in the dream world and leading them to the Dream Machine. The Dream Machine world is composed of six scenes where Dreamers interact with each other and objects, explore colorful worlds filled with choices, and immerse themselves in virtual performances. A place to seep up the wisdom of the ancestors and look to the dawn of tomorrow. The thirty-minute experience culminates in a VR concert led by guitar legend Vernon Reid. (Additional performances by George Clinton, Laurie Anderson, and Skin.)

Next, *Empire at Sea* by Peter Flaherty. *Empire at Sea* is a Solarpunk, multiparticipant, interactive AR drama series set in a futuristic city at sea that tells a father-daughter story addressing themes of climate change, sustainability, multicultural communities, matriarchal lineage, and the conflict between inclusionary and exclusionary social principles in the form of an immersive, room-scale installation with immersive AR headsets and as an app for at-home audiences.

MK: What tips, insights, or advice do you have for future makers and experience designers or storytellers?

KS: The best advice I can give to future makers and designers and storytellers of experiences is to always remember that you are a meaning maker, not just a technologist or a designer of mechanics. The best work I've ever seen is when the technology or the novelty of the design innovation is invisible or a secondary component of the experience. Try to distinguish between the means and the ends, even if the goal is emergence and process over outcome.

When I was in theater school, I was terrified of being a bad actor. I remember going to see plays or films and people saying things like "The acting was horrendous" or "They could have cast a better actor for the lead." I remember thinking, "Agghh! I don't want people to say that about me." I was insecure because I didn't even know how people decided on what was bad acting, it seemed so subjective. One day I realized the answer. When I am aware of the actors being aware of themselves on stage, that is bad acting. When I'm just aware of the character in the story or experience, that is good acting. It's the same with experience design. When the participant is more aware of the mechanics than the intended experience, you may need to reconsider the design. Caveat, sometimes the intention is to make the mechanics, the technology, and the innovation the story.

*"Sometimes reality is too complex.
Stories give it form."*

— Jean-Luc Godard, film director
and screenwriter

6

THE THEORY BEHIND A
SUCCESSFUL EXPERIENCE

|||||||||||||||||||||||||||||||||||||||||||||||||||||||||||||||||||||||||||||||||||||||||||||||||||||||||||||||

WHEN YOU WRITE FROM the participant's perspective, you put yourself in your guest's shoes. You create not from the creator's POV (which is a more detached perspective) but from the perspective of the people who are going to visit, experience, and play in your space. This hones your ability to be empathetic to the participant's experience. You imagine what it would feel like to experience what you are designing for them. You consider all of the factors, physical and psychological, so that you can prioritize your participant's comfort and enjoyment.

I discussed level-setting in chapter 5. We do this in both gaming and immersive experiences so we can set expectations for the player or participant to ensure they feel comfortable and engaged from the moment they begin. The first rule of level-setting is to create a safe, comfortable place so that your participants feel like they have their basic physiological and safety needs met before they engage in play. Consider the fact that you can't fully enjoy yourself knowing that you need to use the restroom, want to grab something to eat, or feel too hot or too cold. You must meet your participant's most basic physiological needs and safety before you can move up Maslow's hierarchy of needs.

Once all of their basic needs are met, the participant is ready to play and be empowered. Unleashing the power of player agency gives meaningful control to the participant in an experience. Notice I use the word "meaningful" rather than "total" or "absolute" to describe their level of control, because the world will still

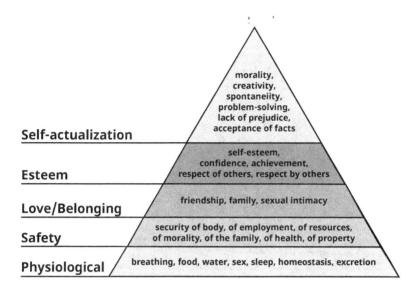

have rules they must follow. These rules are necessary so that every participant or player understands their limitations and boundaries for play.

CRAFTING A COHERENT NARRATIVE

I participated in a fireside chat followed by a Q&A session where an audience member asked, "Is it important to explain the story to the participant? Don't you want the participant to figure it out for themselves or interpret it for themselves?" It's a good question.

Why is it important for your participants to perceive the intended meaning of your experience? Because as a spatial designer, you create meaning via a multisensory, multidimensional environment. If you're creating narrative for art's sake, then perhaps your story would be better served by a different medium, such as a piece in a gallery, a self-published zine, or an experimental film. As an abstract artist, you wouldn't need to make sense of the piece for the observer. You leave it up to the audience to interpret the meaning. It can be as abstract as you want it to be.

A modern art gallery in Downtown Los Angeles. Photo by Margaret Kerrison.

When you visit a modern art gallery, you'll probably see art that you don't recognize or can't easily interpret. The galleries have different ways to help you understand the art (through audio guides, labels, pamphlets, and docents). When an artist creates art, it's a way for them to express themselves and perhaps their state of mind and their perspective of the world, and you'll most likely look to the artist's personal statement or the curator's labels to interpret what you're seeing. Still, the art itself isn't necessarily created for the viewer's understanding. It may be created for the viewer's appreciation, but art is, more often than not, subjective. What one viewer describes as beautiful may be less appealing to another viewer.

In designing spaces and environments, creators should attempt to define the meaning behind the narrative to create a compelling story-based experience that is understood by the audience or participant.

As human beings, we tell stories for many reasons, but for creators of immersive experiences, stories are meant to help us make sense of the world. We make sense of the world by using all of our senses. Without clear intention behind the application of sensory elements, the participants will feel unsafe, lost, confused, and frustrated. They don't know *why* they're experiencing something. There has to be a clear understanding behind their decision-making and actions, or they'll lose interest and emotional investment in the story and outcome. Without understanding the WHY (why am I doing this) and WHAT (what is this place about?), your participants won't care about HOW your experience is manifested. As a result, they miss out on the opportunity to be transformed by your experience.

This is why writers for theme parks and immersive experiences should study narratology, a term coined by Bulgarian French historian and philosopher Tzvetan Todorov. Narratology involves the study of narrative structures and the ways that these affect human perception.[18] It helps us look at how stories are put together and what they *mean*. We use this lens to understand how stories work, how they're made, and what they're trying to say.

When it comes to video games, narratology helps us see how games use elements like characters, plots, and storytelling to make the game more interesting and immersive. It looks at how these elements are communicated and how they make the game *feel* to the player. In other words, it's an intentional approach to crafting a cohesive and engaging narrative structure that guides the visitor's experience and evokes specific emotions, thoughts, or reactions. The best kind of narrative design invites everyone to play.

Narratology seeks to identify and examine the fundamental principles and devices that underlie the creation and understanding of narratives. It attempts to answer the question of whether all forms of narrative can share a framework that helps storytellers create and share their intended meaning with the participant, and it seeks to understand how all of these elements combined affect human perception.

As Hayden White, an American historian, writes, "Far from being one code among many that a culture may utilize for endowing

---

[18] https://www.cla.purdue.edu/academic/english/theory/narratology/modules/intro-duction.html

experience with meaning, narrative is a meta-code, a human universal on the basis of which transcultural messages about the nature of a shared reality can be transmitted."[19] This statement suggests that narrative is not merely one of many communication codes used by cultures to give meaning to an experience. Instead, as a meta-code, it is a universal human phenomenon that serves as a foundational framework for conveying messages about the shared nature of reality across cultures. In other words, narratives are seen as a fundamental and innate aspect of human communication, through which people from diverse backgrounds can transmit and understand complex ideas and concepts that reflect their collective understanding of the world. This perspective highlights the central role of storytelling in human culture and emphasizes its power to bridge cultural divides and convey universal truths about the human experience.

The study of narratology focuses on how participants engage with and interpret narratives, and how the roles of cultural and historical contexts shape these interpretations. Certain references, symbols, metaphors, or themes that are familiar and meaningful in one context might be obscure or hold different connotations in another. This can lead to varying interpretations and responses to the same narrative, depending on the participant's cultural and historical perspective. So your intended meaning may not be interpreted in the same way by different audience members or participants.

Legendary Imagineer Joe Rohde explained to me how he sees plot compared to narrative:

> A lot of people in our business confuse narrative with linear plot. Plot is an armature for narrative. Plot is like a grid, and you put the right things into that grid. It's just like an architectural plot. The word means the same thing, it's the armature, a printout of things, but the narrative

---

[19] Hayden White, *The Content of the Form: Narrative Discourse and Historical Representation.*

itself is not the line. The narrative is the correlation. The legible meaningful correlation of the things that we know is a story. Story has interior meaning that I follow because I can see it coming together, but I don't have to see it coming together in a line of time-based narrative. I can see it coming together. More like the way Chinese writing comes together. I just look at that word and I know that that word has something to do with forest, water, mountain, just from how it's written. It has immediate narrative impact. And spatial design is more like that. The narrative is not written in sequence. It's read in aggregate.[20]

As I said earlier: If you're creating art for art's sake, by all means, don't feel the need to interpret your art to your participant. But if you're creating an immersive experience, you, as the designer, should absolutely know what you're creating. As a designer, your INTENT must be UNDERSTOOD. If not, your participant will wonder, "Why did I just do that? What was *that* all about? What does it all mean? What's the point? Why did I spend any time and money on this? I don't think I'll ever return."

As human beings, we are pattern seekers, connecting the dots and quickly making sense of things. As storytellers, it is our superpower to create meaning and order in an otherwise chaotic world.

It's important to note that your participants may walk away with slightly different interpretations and impressions of your experience, but ultimately, they should all agree on what the experience is about based on how they FEEL. As Joe Rohde said, it must have "immediate narrative impact."

There are experiences, like Meow Wolf, in which the full narrative can be difficult to grasp for most visitors. Like when we play a game, Meow Wolf offers different levels of engagement. If visitors

---

[20] This interview was conducted by Margaret Kerrison on May 15, 2023.

are completionists, they will dedicate all of their time and energy to finding all of the clues and uncovering all of the mysteries and interactive elements, as was intended by the designers. Completionists aim to fully explore and experience all content, complete every objective, collect all items or achievements, and unlock every secret within a game. They derive satisfaction from meticulously exploring every corner of the game world, overcoming every challenge, and attaining all available rewards.

However, I would guess that the majority of Meow Wolf's visitors simply enjoy the experience at its face value, not grasping the full meaning or intention of the storytelling. There is some value in feeling lost or surprised for a moment, but as a whole, you want every visitor to walk away feeling like they have experienced something memorable and transformative.

Ultimately, an experience should be designed with different levels of engagement for your visitor. Designers should demonstrate a dedicated and informed intention to engage their visitors in the experience. It shouldn't be random or spontaneous, if you can help it. There will be plenty of opportunities for visitors or users to find their own way of engaging with your experience, but ultimately,

Meow Wolf's Convergence Station, Denver, CO. Photo by Margaret Kerrison.

as a designer, your role is to design for a purpose. You must create the foundation of your experience before visitors and users naturally add to, deviate from, and change it based on their preferred levels of engagement.

Narratology is a tool all of us creators and storytellers can use because it provides a structured framework for understanding the mechanics and impact of storytelling. It helps all creatives in crafting compelling narratives and understanding how different techniques can influence audience engagement and emotional resonance.

Types of Narratology in Games

What are the different types of narratology in games? It depends on who you ask. Henry Jenkins III, a respected scholar and professor at the University of Southern California, describes in his short piece "Game Design as Narrative Architecture" four types of narratives: Evocative Spaces, Enacting Stories, Embedded Narratives, and Emergent Narratives.[21]

Chris Stone, a veteran video game developer, outlined four different main types of narratives: linear, string of pearls, branching, and amusement park.[22]

I'll keep the terms simple, but I see five basic forms of storytelling in games that can be applied to physical immersive experiences. I want to share all of them with you so you can think about how you can be more creative in your options. Ultimately, you want to consider how each form of storytelling can be applied to your immersive experience. By thinking about the possibilities, perhaps you may find a form that is best suited for your story.

LINEAR NARRATIVES

Linear narratives follow a fixed, predetermined sequence of events, much like a traditional story in media such as books or movies.

---

[21] https://web.mit.edu/~21fms/People/henry3/games&narrative.html
[22] https://www.gamedeveloper.com/design/the-evolution-of-video-games-as-a-storytelling-medium-and-the-role-of-narrative-in-modern-games

The Haunted Mansion, Disneyland, Anaheim, CA. Photo by Margaret Kerrison.

Players progress through the game in a set order, and the plot unfolds in a linear fashion with a clear beginning, middle, and end.

Examples of linear narrative games include *The Last of Us* and *Tomb Raider* series. For immersive experiences, most of the rides we know and love, like Pirates of the Caribbean and the Haunted Mansion, follow this model.

Nonlinear Narratives

Nonlinear narratives offer players choices and branching paths that affect the outcome of the story. The player's decisions can lead to different storylines and multiple endings. This type of narratology allows for player agency and a more personalized gaming experience. The game adapts its story based on the player's decisions, creating a stronger sense of urgency and immersion. Examples of nonlinear narrative games include *Her Story* and *Life Is Strange*.

Immersive experiences like *Sleep No More* and *Star Wars*: Galactic Starcruiser attempt to follow this model. However, neither of these experiences are completely nonlinear, as they both have branching paths but do not offer multiple endings.

OPEN-WORLD NARRATIVES

Open-world narratives provide players with a sandbox-like environment and freedom to create their own stories within the context of the world. These games offer little or no fixed plot and instead encourage players to explore and create their own narratives. *Minecraft* and the *Grand Theft Auto* series are examples of games with open-world narratives.

teamLab in Tokyo and Singapore. Photos by Margaret Kerrison.

Animal Crossing is a game my family and many others discovered in lockdown during the COVID-19 pandemic. It gave us a chance to explore a world without any particular goal or mission. For that period of time when we felt trapped and isolated, it was a great way for us to feel like we could escape and visit our family and friends via their online islands. Open-world narratives are one of my favorite types of games. They can be relaxing, meditative, and freeing. They're a wonderful form of escapism.

Places like teamLab and Meow Wolf have attempted to create this very complex model. I look forward to seeing more of this model manifested in the real world.

Environmental Storytelling

Environmental storytelling involves using the game world's environment, level design, and in-game objects to convey narrative information. Instead of relying heavily on cutscenes (the noninteractive in-game cinematic sequences that advance the game's storyline, provide context, or showcase important events) and dialogue, this type of narratology allows players to discover the story through exploration and observation. Games like *Journey* and *Gone Home* use environmental storytelling effectively. (As a side note, cutscenes are used differently in immersive experiences. They come in the form of transitions that bridge one room or scene and the next. They may be intentionally designed, such as a scene you witness in digital or physical format, or they may simply be functional, such as stairs you have to climb, a bridge you walk over, a tunnel you go into, a hallway to walk through, and more.)

Theme park attractions often use environmental storytelling. When you think about how the queues and rides are designed, oftentimes you don't see a character. The environment tells the story through visuals, audio, and sometimes smell and touch. Storytelling is told mainly through the environment instead. Immersive experiences like Scout Expedition Co's. *The Nest* and Meow Wolf follow this model.

Episodic Narratives

Episodic-narrative games release content in episodes, similar to a TV series. Each individual episode may have its story arc, but together they are interconnected to create an overarching narrative. Telltale Games like *The Walking Dead* and *The Wolf Among Us* series follow this format.

I'm excited to see this manifest in the form of immersive storytelling in the real world. Imagine if a company creates this kind of shared narrative in their universe, where each physical venue is a chapter of a larger story, revealed in an episodic format. Consider how episodic narratives in traditional media are, more often than not, sequential. Imagine how a series of physical places could be experienced in a logical order to create a sense of narrative coherence and urgency.

Ultimately, choosing the ideal storytelling format for your immersive experience is a subjective decision. There isn't a definitive right or wrong approach. You need to consider your story, its intended meaning, and its style of gameplay. Think about your participants' actions and how they could achieve a profound sense of agency and immersion within your narrative.

I want to delve deeper into creating an open-world narrative, a "sandbox" for your participants to feel welcomed into and immersed in your world. Why is this important to discuss before immediately jumping into what your world looks like? Because your world can be the most immersive and interactive world by design, but without the proper invitation to play and a call to action in the context of your world, there's no REASON for them to want to interact with your world. Give your participants the motivation, the desire, and the fulfillment to WANT to interact and play with your world.

The concept of a "sandbox" in the context of playing games and engaging in immersive experiences refers to an open and unstructured environment that allows players or participants to explore, experiment, and create within the confines of the world. It's a space where individuals have a high degree of freedom and agency to shape their experience and interactions, often without strict objectives or predefined goals.

The term draws an analogy to the idea of playing in a physical sandbox, where children can shape and build various structures without a predetermined outcome. They are free to play and engage as they wish, with no obligations or expectations. Sandbox games (such as *Minecraft* and Roblox) and immersive experiences have a high replay value because participants can return and create something new with each visit.

teamLab, the international art collective, creates a sandbox beautifully in their work. In their own words, "Their collaborative practice seeks to navigate the confluence of art, science, technology, and the natural world. Through art, the interdisciplinary group of specialists, including artists, programmers, engineers, CG animators, mathematicians, and architects, aims to explore the relationship between the self and the world, and new forms of perception."[23]

Whether you're coloring a fish to scan and drop into their *Sketch Aquarium: Connected World* installation or balancing on swinging colorful beams or playing with giant interactive light-up balls, there's a big welcome and invitation to play for guests of all ages and abilities.

teamLab creates a beautiful, engaging sandbox world where people want to join and play, cocreate, and contribute to the larger art, socialize in physical, multisensory worlds that challenge them, and see themselves in the art. Their collective is so successful that they continue to open in multiple locations around the world, many with unique, site-specific experiences.

I can imagine a stunning sandbox experience inspired by one of my favorite games, *Monument Valley*, by ustwo Games. This

---

[23] https://www.teamlab.art/about/

game is "a surreal exploration through fantastical architecture and impossible geometry. The player guides the silent princess Ida through mysterious monuments, to uncover hidden paths, unfold optical illusions and outsmart the enigmatic Crow People."[24] I'd love to go into this M.C. Escher–like world and solve the many puzzles to reveal new paths and destinations.

I'd also like to visit a sandbox experience in which I can encounter different puzzle-solving escape rooms inspired by the fun, eerie, and surrealistic games by Rusty Lake, like the *Cube Escape* and *Rusty Lake* collection. It would feel like being inside a modern, immersive interpretation of a Salvador Dalí painting.

The important elements of a successful sandbox experience include freedom and exploration, player agency, creativity and self-expression, experimentation, community building, bonding, and the exciting possibilities of emergent gameplay. In a sandbox, emergent gameplay occurs when unscripted and unplanned interactions between game mechanics, objects, and player actions lead to unexpected outcomes. This can result in unique and memorable experiences that are not explicitly designed by the creators.

GENRES AND SUBGENRES

There are so many different kinds of games, and they're all constantly evolving and overlapping with one another. That's why "gaming" is such a broad term. Games are designed to provide players with various experiences, from action-packed adventures and strategic challenges to creative environmental simulations and social interactions. Players interact with a virtual environment that immediately responds in real time, providing feedback and presenting new challenges or objectives. "Real time" is the key term, so that the player's actions are immediately experienced. There's an immediacy to gaming that makes a player feel alive and in the

---

[24] https://ustwo.com/work/monument-valley/

moment. When completing a level, vanquishing a villain or boss, rescuing someone, figuring out a puzzle, and more, the stakes feel significant. They feel urgent and, more frequently than not, time dependent.

And with so many different games, there's a genre for everyone. Personally, I prefer action-adventure, exploration, interactive fiction, puzzle, music and rhythm, and tower-defense, real-time strategy games, although there are some games in other genres that occasionally surprise me. It's good to try different genres to see which ones resonate with you the most. Playing different games will expose you to various kinds of storytelling.

Immersive Experience Genres and Subgenres

Much like the ever-evolving world of gaming, immersive experiences are quickly expanding and diversifying, spawning their own distinct genres and subgenres.

As a result, pinning down a precise definition for an immersive experience is becoming increasingly challenging. It must combine a multitude of components to craft a storytelling platform, employing a diverse array of tools and techniques, all in the pursuit of conveying the most captivating and emotionally resonant narrative. These experiences can manifest in various forms, such as participatory theater, mazelike discovery realms, interactive rides, immersive adventures, or indoor environments that transport you to another world. Ultimately, it falls upon the creator to identify the ideal form that will effectively captivate the participant and convey the intended message of the story.

CREATING A COHESIVE GAMEPLAY

A player or participant's actions must make sense in the context of their character, story, and world.

For example, a participant shouldn't be involved in a first-person shooter gameplay when the world has nothing to do with that action. In gaming, this conflict is called ludonarrative dissonance,[25] which refers to the conflict between a game's narrative elements and its gameplay mechanics. The term "ludonarrative dissonance" was coined by video game designer and writer Clint Hocking when he introduced the concept in a blog post in 2007 while discussing the game *BioShock*. Hocking wrote:

> To cut straight to the heart of it, Bioshock seems to suffer from a powerful dissonance between what it is about as a game, and what it is about as a story. By throwing the narrative and ludic elements of the work into opposition, the game seems to openly mock the player for having believed in the fiction of the game at all. The leveraging of the game's narrative structure against its ludic structure all but destroys the player's ability to feel connected to either, forcing the player to either abandon the game in protest (which I almost did) or simply accept that the game cannot be enjoyed as both a game and a story, and to then finish it for the mere sake of finishing it.

In other words, the narrative and gameplay should always support one another and be in the same context. They should adhere and align with the world's theme, narrative, and rules, so participants don't question why they are there or what they are doing.

In theme parks and other immersive experiences, there are many ways the gameplay and actions of the participants might not align with the narrative. For example, imagine a VR game that takes place in an alternative future where the city is plagued by an alien invasion. Players are tasked with using critical thinking skills and strategies to scavenge for resources, form alliances, and ultimately survive in this postapocalyptic world. The game's narrative

---

[25] https://clicknothing.typepad.com/click_nothing/2007/10/ludonarrative-d.html

sets a grim and intense tone, emphasizing the struggle for survival and the emotional weight of the situation.

However, when the participants begin the experience, they find themselves in the gameplay mechanics of simple, continuous arcade-style shooting sequences in which players eliminate hordes of aliens with little to no challenge. The gameplay mechanics don't match the emotional gravity of the narrative. Instead of feeling the urgency and desperation to survive in this postapocalyptic world, participants feel more like a detached player mindlessly mashing buttons to vanquish their enemies.

This is a clear example of ludonarrative dissonance because the narrative's deeply serious tone is at odds with the gameplay mechanics. As a result, the desired emotions are not effectively communicated through the experience. This dissonance makes it more challenging for participants to fully immerse and engage with the world and find motivation to engage in a superficial, button-mashing gameplay.

In designing your experience, it's important to remind yourself that the physical and interactive design elements of your experience are important, but so are the emotional and social design elements. You must plan beforehand and be intentional in the qualitative aspects of your experience so that your participants won't feel lost, frustrated, or confused. You have to design the gameplay for their wish fulfillment and emotional takeaway.

JUMP-STARTER QUESTIONS

- What narrative style best suits your visitors' engagement with your experience? How do the gameplay and story support one another?
- What emotional takeaway does your experience aim to convey, and how do the audience's actions contribute to that meaning?

CUTSCENE: AN INTERVIEW WITH WENDY McCLELLAN ANDERSON[26]

Director of IP Creative at Riot Games, former executive creative director of Walt Disney Imagineering

MK: Can you describe your role at Riot Games?

WMA: Before I was hired at Riot Games, they spun up an entertainment division, which is focused on film, television, and animation, alongside other things like music and consumer products. They have a very linear storytelling platform sitting next to the games, which don't exist within any story, really. But the players really love the power fantasy of each champion that they play. So if you play *League of Legends*, the stories of the champions you're playing are compelling. So it's a challenge when you've got one team that's working on linear narrative and another team that needs to make gameplay work. How do you marry these two things? And how do you think about a future in which they can peacefully coexist and enhance one another? So that's what I was brought in to do. I'm looking at the landscape of what Riot is putting out there and asking: What else can we do? How do we create the strategies and structures in which our storytelling is cohesive and exciting for players and builds fandom? We actually just announced to players a couple of weeks ago that we're working toward a future where it's one cohesive world.

MK: What guiding principles does Riot Games follow in their storytelling?

WMA: We talk a lot about the world and core truths of the characters. *League of Legends* is competitive gameplay. It's the largest esport in the world. If you took the NBA, smashed it with capture

---

[26] This interview was conducted by Margaret Kerrison over video chat. The transcript was edited for clarity and length.

the flag, and put a layer of fantasy over it, that's *League of Legends*. The players are very invested in that competitive gameplay. We introduce new champions every year into the game, so at this point we have like 167 champions. So imagine if *Star Wars* had 167 Skywalkers. It's a lot to manage. But what makes a champion really resonate for players is the question of: Are they really playable? Am I going to win the game with them? Can I show off something? Can I learn something cool and new? Sometimes it's, Do they have an awesome backstory? But how they look and play in the game is the majority of it.

MK: So you have a background in theater, and then you went into storytelling and live entertainment for theme parks. And now you're in games. How do those experiences relate to what you're doing today?

WMA: I have a classical theater background. I was trained in Shakespeare and the Greeks, and I love them still to this day, but I was dissatisfied with them, because I'm dissatisfied with the passive experience. So as a theater director, I would go into theaters and take the seats out and, you know, make the audience stand in a cocktail party to watch *Antigone* unfold. Back in the day, I think they would have called it site-specific theater. Now it's just immersive. But I think anybody who's got that storytelling brain that asks how they can get people excited about a world and the people that populate that world, and get them to the point where it's aspirational for them to invest in that world and play in that world in their minds — that translates across any medium.

I'm looking for these opportunities that ask, How can we leverage this world for fifteen to twenty years? Instead of a singular story, how can we create an opportunity for multiple teams to leverage the same obstacle, theme, or environment for ten years of storytelling? So it's sort of broadened how I think. I still leverage the storytelling expertise that I developed working on *Much Ado About Nothing*, which is essentially finding the spine of a story and seeing how you can follow it and get people motivated to drive toward that same action. I'm still doing that, but now I'm thinking about it in terms of worlds and multiplicity instead of one singular arc.

MK: How do you think about the player experience?

WMA: When you're playing a game like *League of Legends*, it takes about an hour to play a full game, and there's something about the thrill of the gameplay. So with PC games like *League*, it's all about that adrenaline rush of the competition in the game. That's not about a linear narrative. When I play a game that's got a through line like *The Last of Us*, I might play not just for beating the game but for the story and the nature of how I'm moving through the world and the exploration of the people that I want to meet. So they have very different intentions. But what I am excited about is that I can play an hour of *League* and then I can go watch *Arcane* and really dive deep into the world. And what we're building is how to continue to give people ways to dive deeper into the world. It might be a book, comic, another game. It might be a buffet of experiences. Or whatever I feel is closest to my excitement and what's going to get me invested.

MK: How do you make stories meaningful for your players and audiences?

WMA: When I worked at a very traditional theater, I was never satisfied with the lights going down and a group of people having a passive experience. So I was constantly doing stuff, like making everybody attend a play that starts in a park and ends in an old warehouse. I gave the audience some agency for how they experienced the play.

I think seeing the magician David Copperfield in Las Vegas might have been one of the few times that I was like, "oh, I have no idea how they did it." I want people to be so engaged and invested emotionally that they're not looking for how it happens. And that only happens when I am deeply invested in the story that's unfolding. I want there to be some piece of it that is reflective of an experience that I understand. It's about empathy and permission to be you at your highest self. And no one's going to judge you. It's a safe space in which to experiment.

I'm interested in painting a world that we want to be in. Like we did with *Star Wars*: Galactic Starcruiser, I'm interested in creating things that really connect people with their loved ones on this journey and feel a sense of "I'm a hero in my own story. I'm the hero in my family now." I'll never forget the first time my daughter met Rey in *Star Wars*: Galaxy's Edge. Rey sent her on a mission, and she stood up taller and was engaged in a way that made her braver. It's being able to imbue people with a part of themselves that hasn't been active before or hasn't had the opportunity to show up before. It's a sort of catharsis.

Everyone accepts you. All of these strangers come together and accept each other as they come into the story, on an emotionally resonant journey together. The difference in the experience that we built with the starcruiser is that you're actually engaged and playing together and creating this fiction together. There's real power in that deep acceptance. You may never see any of those people again. Some of them may become lifelong friendships. I know that there have been guests that met people on these journeys that they have kept in touch with. It was deeply life-changing for them. To allow parts of themselves that they've been hiding to show up, and to not let go even when they leave. I know, it's crazy to say, but we change lives with this kind of storytelling.

MK: What advice do you have for future designers and storytellers?

WMA: The first thing is keep in mind: the heart. The core is the warmth and the connection that you're trying to create, which is usually the heart of the experience. And the second thing is it's okay to do less and not plan it all. Doing less means giving people the space to participate.

"For me, that emotional payoff is what it's all about. I want you to laugh or cry when you read a story . . . or do both at the same time. I want your heart, in other words. If you want to learn something, go to school."

— Stephen King, author

7

EMOTIONAL PAYOFF AND MEANINGFUL CONSEQUENCES

Y OUR JOB AS A DESIGNER isn't simply to create a world where you can give your players or participants agency to do whatever they want and be done with your work. You have to ensure that the consequences really do matter and that it all feeds into a big emotional payoff. In other words, you need to make your participants feel like they *earned* their emotional payoff. You have to strike a delicate balance. There has to be enough of a challenge to keep participants motivated, but not too much of a challenge that you cause hopelessness and frustration. And if you're dealing with younger audiences, you definitely don't want them to fail.

When you play a game, you have the opportunity to improve your skills and to earn badges, rewards, objects, and weapons when you vanquish your opponents. You have to earn your way to new levels, bosses or villains, and other narrative paths. So how can you do that in physical immersive experiences?

Netflix's Squid Game: The Trials experience ran for only a few months in Los Angeles and was a brilliant example of how to incorporate gaming into a physical experience. In the Netflix series, contestants compete for a large sum of money to be the last contestant standing, with everyone else facing death. How can a designer transform such a dark concept into something fun and engaging? The Netflix team did an excellent job not only drawing inspiration from the series's games but also incorporating unique games that would resonate with an American audience, such as a large-scale version of the board game Operation as well as a final game inspired by the egg-and-spoon race. (Side note: I was one of the last two remaining and both our eggs fell at the same time, but the Front Man randomly chose the other contestant. Boo.)

The idea of having a group of contestants go through a series of games, accumulating points to be tallied at the end of each round, and displaying the scores on the digital board at the beginning of every game really pushed us to do better in the next round. Our competitive spirits were ignited, and we were completely engrossed. The games were a mix of mental and physical challenges and often included a social aspect as well, such as when we were divided into teams and played a large-scale version of the Battleship board game, requiring us to communicate and strategize together. Even though we were competing against each other, we bonded, cheered on strangers, and genuinely wanted to see everyone succeed. Overall, it was a great example of turning gaming into a social and physically immersive experience. I was fully engaged and present for the entire seventy minutes of gameplay. Even if participants had never watched *Squid Game* on Netflix (one of my friends had not), they still had a memorable time playing the game.

Each visit to an immersive experience should be great as standalone experiences, complete in itself. If you want to create a permanent experience, remember that the first visit is crucial; it should leave a lasting impression so that visitors will be compelled to return again and again. Consider how you can create enjoyment in the first, second, and subsequent visits. How do you create purpose and meaningful consequences in every visit? Can you reward participants for completing all of the adventures and activities? How can you make it feel earned? Consider how to make your adventures challenging and compelling enough, but not too difficult or confusing to follow.

Video games do this well by giving players the agency to make choices to complete a mission as players encounter characters that they grow to care about and immerse themselves in a rich, complex world. How can you apply some of these practices to creating your immersive experiences? How do you create visitor attachment to your experience when they're not familiar with your world or story? Or if your guests *are* familiar with the story and IP, how can you meet and exceed their expectations? In other words, how do you make your guests fall in love with your story regardless of their level of fandom or attachment to the brand?

Visitor attachment to an experience refers to the emotional connection, engagement, and lasting impact that an individual develops as a result of interacting with a particular event, place, or activity. It involves nostalgia and positive feelings that an individual associates with the experience. In its best form, the visitor feels like they have an important place in your experience — that they belong. **They feel welcomed, included, valued, and empowered**.

Consider this perspective as a designer — the WINDOW or lens through which you can craft a genuinely emotionally captivating immersive world that will foster a strong visitor attachment. Keep in mind the acronym V.I.E.W. as you look through the window:

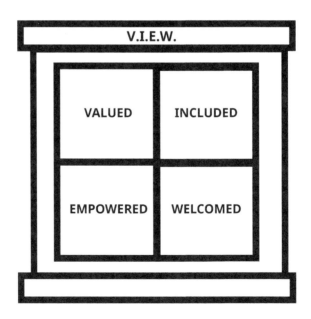

- *V* for *Valued*: This refers to your visitor feeling recognized and appreciated for their contributions, qualities, or presence. When someone feels valued, they believe that their opinions, efforts, and presence are important and respected by others. They feel like they are seen, heard, useful, and, eventually, masterful.

- *I* for *Included*: Feeling included means being part of a group, community, or environment in a way that makes a person feel accepted, involved, and not left out. It's the sense of being embraced as a member rather than being excluded or isolated. Who hasn't felt left out before? When your immersive space is designed well, this powerful feeling will guarantee visitor attachment to your brand and experience.

- *E* for *Empowered*: To be empowered means to feel confident, capable, and in control of one's own actions and decisions. It often involves your visitor having the ability to make choices, take initiative, and effect change in their path or circumstances. This relates to the power of agency, which we'll discuss again in a later chapter.

- *W* for *Welcomed*: A check-in person at the beginning of your experience doesn't count as an emotionally engaging welcome. Consider how you *feel* when you enter the home of a loved one or good friend. You immediately feel SEEN and HEARD, even TOUCHED with a handshake, kisses, or a hug. When someone feels welcomed, they experience a sense of warmth, acceptance, and hospitality from others. It means being greeted and received with openness and friendliness that they don't normally (or ever) experience anywhere else.

Does your experience make your visitor feel all of these emotional states of being?

When visitors feel attached to the immersive environment, they are more likely to engage deeply with the content, become emotionally involved in the story or scenario, and have a stronger sense of presence and purpose within the world. This attachment can lead to a more profound and memorable experience, as well as increased levels of immersion and engagement.

GUIDING THE EXPERIENCE TOWARD AN EMOTIONAL PAYOFF

I fully acknowledge that creating an immersive land where visitors feel like they have an integral role to play with a sense of agency isn't easy to accomplish in a physical environment where there are multiple "players" in the world. This is one of the greatest challenges in creating a physical immersive experience.

With that said, here are some ways to create meaningful consequences with great emotional payoff:

EMOTIONAL PAYOFF
MIND MAP

TIME PRESSURE AND SENSE OF URGENCY

CHARACTER RELATIONSHIPS

CHOICES AND BRANCHING NARRATIVES

MORAL DILEMMAS

EMOTIONAL PAYOFF

FORESHADOWING

PERSONALIZATION

NOSTALGIA

REFLECTION AND CLOSURE

Time Pressure and Sense of Urgency
Gaming demonstrates this storytelling technique best. Introduce time-sensitive situations that force players to make quick

decisions. The pressure can enhance emotional intensity and the feeling of consequence. Can you solve the puzzle in two minutes? Who chooses to go into the creepy dungeon alone? Who chooses to pull the lever covered with spiders to save the group from being crushed by a falling ceiling? Dialing in on the sense of urgency creates higher stakes for your participants. It's also a really effective way for them to be present and in the moment because they understand the exact amount of time they need to focus and complete a task or goal. Escape rooms are a great example of this model. Try to solve all of the puzzles before your time runs out.

Character Relationships

Develop well-rounded and relatable NPCs that participants can connect with emotionally. Players' actions and choices should have a significant impact on the storyline and outcomes. Develop meaningful relationships between characters that can evolve based on participant interactions. Participants should feel invested in the growth of these relationships and care about their outcomes. Create complex, multilayered characters that allow participants to empathize and see themselves in the narrative. When participants identify with the characters, their emotional investment in the story and experience increases.

At Imagineering, we train the Cast Members to be a part of the themed land they are working in so that they may have meaningful interactions with the guests. Obviously, there are live entertainment characters walking around every once in a while, but never forget that the regular staff want the opportunity to play and engage with guests too.

Choices and Branching Narratives

Introduce meaningful choices that affect the direction of the experience. Ensure that these choices are impactful and lead to distinct consequences. This encourages participants to invest emotionally in their decisions. By establishing a clear cause-and-effect relationship between the actions of the participants and the outcomes within the experience, they see the direct results of their decisions, which enhances their sense of agency and emotional investment.

Gaming is all about real-time consequences based on the player's actions. How can your experience create similar real-time consequences based on participant interaction? Design interactions, from quick, small wins to big, impactful ones, that allow participants to directly influence the environment or characters. The feeling of agency contributes to a stronger emotional connection.

For example, in the immersive participatory theater experience *Sleep No More*, you can choose which character to follow, which room to explore, and which direction you want to walk in. As if in a real-life video game, you are meant to explore and discover different scenes to make sense of the deconstructed story of *Macbeth*. Your experience is a nonlinear, multibranching narrative world that guarantees a different experience with each visit. There are certain scenes that all of the visitors observe as participants, but where you decide to go and how long you decide to stay in a scene or room is up to you.

Moral Dilemmas

I personally love this storytelling technique. Present participants with ethical or moral dilemmas that require them to make difficult choices. The emotional impact comes from the weight of their decisions and the consequences that follow. When a moral dilemma is combined with a surprise or twist, it makes the story more compelling. Include moments when characters experience loss or make sacrifices. Will you make decisions about who in your group should go into the dark woods to retrieve the object? Will you choose which person to save? When executed effectively, these moments can create strong emotional reactions.

For example, I experienced one serial killer–themed escape room in which we had to send two people from our group into a dark, confined space to help "navigate" the rest of the group to where we could find the next clue without the ability to see where we were. There was a map that they could use to shout out instructions to the rest of the group, but they couldn't see the room we were standing in. We had to choose two people who were effective communicators and also not afraid of being confined in a small, dark space.

In that same escape room experience, we later had to choose one person to go into a dark creepy closet, which had a secret tunnel to the next room. She courageously went into the closet, not knowing there was a very scary character waiting for her in the connecting room. It was frightening, to say the least, because we saw her appear in a grainy feed of a black-and-white TV monitor that turned on at the opportune time. Did we just sacrifice our brave friend? Spoiler: She was fine.

Foreshadowing

One of the oldest tricks of storytelling is to set up foreshadowing early in the experience to hint at future events. When those hints pay off later, participants feel a sense of satisfaction and emotional connection. They also feel very clever when they're able to connect the dots later and realize that they should've seen it coming all along. Consider how you can pepper in symbols, dialogue, visuals, and other ways of subconsciously giving the answers to your participants without being direct about it.

Personalization

If you're able, consider tailoring the experience to the individual preferences, choices, and behaviors of the participants. Gaming does this effectively by giving players the ability to choose their own avatars, skins (appearance changes), weapons, and other accessories in addition to choosing their own paths. When participants see their own influence on the story or world, their emotional involvement becomes deepened. This can come in the

Star Wars: Galaxy's Edge, Disneyland, Anaheim, CA. Photo by Margaret Kerrison.

form of choosing a particular character to follow, joining a particular group, or choosing a special theme, like what my team did for participants building lightsabers at Savi's Workshop – Handbuilt Lightsabers in *Star Wars*: Galaxy's Edge. We created four different themes of lighsaber parts (Peace and Justice, Power and Control, Elemental Nature, and Protection and Defense) and the choice of four crystal colors.

Personalization works better with smaller groups so that it maintains its intimacy. Giving your visitors the ability to make choices, even simple ones, goes a long way in contributing to an emotional payoff. Find the perfect balance. You don't want to give people too many choices or they will become overwhelmed. This is a phenomenon called the "paradox of choice," a term that was popularized by the American psychologist Barry Schwartz in his 2004 book titled *The Paradox of Choice: Why More Is Less*. He explores the idea that while having more choices might seem like a good thing, it can lead to increased anxiety, decision fatigue, and a sense of dissatisfaction due to the overwhelming nature of too many options. (This concept was discussed prior to Schwartz, but he popularized it, along with the term.) When the number of choices increases, so does the difficulty of knowing what is best. Instead of increasing our freedom to have what we want, the paradox of choice suggests that having too many choices actually limits our freedom.

Nostalgia

Playing on nostalgia is another great technique. Experiences that trigger nostalgia or evoke sentimental feelings can lead to a stronger attachment, as individuals connect the experience to their personal history. Consider how there are nostalgic moments in our lives that we all share: falling in love, breaking up, feeling left out, moving away from home, connecting with a new friend, being a parent, losing a pet, getting lost, feeling joy. By offering these nostalgic moments, you are very likely going to trigger an emotional response and attachment to your world, giving your visitors an opportunity to perceive and understand your world through the context of their own lives.

teamLab does this beautifully in their works of art around the world. There isn't much explanation given to the visitors when they enter, except for a few rules to follow. However, when visitors enter a space that looks like giant swings, or giant inflatable balloons, or a large digital art canvas, they tap into their childlike selves and, for a moment, can remember what it feels like to be a kid again. teamLab taps into nostalgia so successfully that both children and adults can enjoy their time together.

Reflection and Closure

The best narrative-driven games often have a satisfying emotional payoff at the completion of the game. I remember playing Telltale's *The Walking Dead* season one, for which the entire game I played a character named Lee Everett, a convicted criminal, who rescues and protects an orphaned girl named Clementine. Throughout the game, I connected with Lee based on the decisions that I made.

We barely survived the most horrific situations together, and by the end of the game, I deeply resonated with the character. To my surprise, the game ended with the end of his life, by my hand. I was now in control of Clementine's character and had to make the choice to end Lee's life after he got bitten by a "walker." It was a very satisfying moment of reflection and closure for me as a player.

Physical immersive experiences can learn a lot from gaming storytelling by offering satisfying reflection and closure. Many experiences either make visitors exit through the gift shop or immediately show visitors the door. Where's the space to contemplate and reflect on what they've experienced? Do you really want your visitors to reflect in the exit or parking lot? Provide opportunities for participants to reflect on their choices and the outcomes they've experienced. A sense of closure can lead to a satisfying emotional payoff that will allow the space for the experience to resonate.

PLAYTESTING FOR EMOTIONAL IMPACT

Ultimately, you can make all the plans in the world for a strong emotional impact, but that doesn't mean it's going to land the way you want — and that's why playtesting is so essential. A playtest refers to the process of evaluating and assessing a game or interactive experience by having individuals, often referred to as playtesters, engage with the game to provide feedback and insights. Playtests are conducted during the development phase of a game, whether it's a video game, board game, card game, or any other interactive medium. Did it make your participants feel something? If so, what did they feel? Get their unfiltered, honest opinion. Then iterate, iterate, and iterate, until you get it just right.

Ensure that every participant, no matter who they are, can immediately feel like they belong in your world and story. The reality is that you can't possibly know every backstory of every participant entering your experience, so you must set the status quo and level-set to tell a cohesive emotional story from beginning to end.

In summary, creating meaningful consequences and emotional payoff requires careful planning, attention to detail, and iteration. Balancing these elements within the overall experience can result in a more immersive and emotionally resonant encounter for your players.

JUMP-STARTER QUESTIONS

- What are the consequences in your experience, and how will they be FELT by the participant?
- What will make your experience successful as a stand-alone, regardless of familiarity with the subject matter or story?
- What are the pacing and tension of the experience? How will you design and control these elements?

"A game is the complete exploration of freedom within a restrictive environment."

— Vineet Raj Kapoor, game developer and author

8

THE CHALLENGE OF
SCALING PLAYABILITY

‖‖‖

H OW DO YOU SUCCESSFULLY CREATE an experience for multiple players in a physical environment? There's an added challenge of optimizing guest flow and scaling playability. As many of us in the industry know, the challenge of scaling an immersive experience so that it remains engaging and meaningful to every single visitor is a tough nut to crack.

Many immersive storytellers have taken their shot at how to do this by giving visitors individual games to play on their phones or competing with other groups. The traditional model of theme park rides and attractions works because you have a known number of guests riding at any given time and participants to fill your seats. But how do you effectively create gameplay in an immersive experience where you're giving every participant agency? How can they feel like they have personally affected the outcome of their experience even with other participants involved?

Should the experience be partially personal, like what *Sleep No More* and other interactive experiences do by pulling participants into separate scenes or rooms? Or can there be ways to scale the play so that everyone can experience the same thing and feel the collective energy of being in a sports arena, concert, or parade or fireworks display like in a Disney park or The Sphere Experience?

As a designer, I want to invite and include as many people as possible. In the context of your sandbox, consider how you can create a meaningful immersive experience that still feels engaging and compelling. This might mean lowering the number of participants at a time, breaking them out in groups, or engaging your participants in play through audio or by using another tool.

This interactive aspect of storytelling becomes more challenging as more participants engage in an experience. After all, if every single participant has agency over the outcome of the experience, then whose actions are more dominant and influential in the outcome of the story? There are different ways to approach this method without affecting the gameplay of others. Perhaps a participant goes on an individual journey of choices or a journey with their own group. Or, as the number of participants increases, the story outcome becomes a competition between sides, as in Secret Cinema's Arcane Immersive Experience, based on the video game *League of Legends*. (*League of Legends* was adapted into an animated series on Netflix, which was then adapted into a physical immersive experience.)

When I bought a ticket to the Arcane experience, I was randomly assigned an in-story character to use during my two-hour experience into the Undercity, which was run by Silco, a criminal overlord and architect of an independent Nation of Zaun, along with his enforcer daughter, Jinx.

A multilevel set welcomed participants to freely explore and interact with actors playing characters from the series. Depending on your desired level of engagement, you can choose to enjoy a drink at the bar, go on side missions and do puzzles in two secret rooms, or go all in and join a team to go on missions, like acquiring "shimmer," stealing from other teams, or distributing shimmer throughout the set, which determines a unique climax to the story that changes based on the participants each night. Depending on the amount of shimmer acquired by a team, there's a different winner each time.

I got lost in the immersive world and story, but honestly, I got lost in the motivation to do the missions. Because there were so many people doing the same thing — collecting shimmer — I felt that my actions didn't matter. I experienced a diffusion of responsibility, also known as the "bystander effect," a sociopsychological phenomenon in which a person is less likely to take responsibility for action or inaction when other bystanders or witnesses are present. I felt that with so many other bystanders (or participants), I didn't need to take action. Perhaps they allowed too many people into this experience? With fewer people, I would've enjoyed the experience more.

THE IMPORTANCE OF REPLAY VALUE

The goal of any theme park or immersive experience is to engage your visitors and provide them with lasting memories. Replay value ensures that your visitors have a reason to come back for multiple visits, extending their engagement and creating meaningful memories with the overall experience. You don't always need rides and attractions to increase the replay value of your experience. Rides are fun because they provide instant gratification for all ages and you can't replicate the experience anywhere else (unless you go to another theme park). So if you don't have rides in your experience, you'll have to appeal to your audience in other ways.

Consider offering a variety of different elements, storylines, outcomes, or interactive features within an experience to keep visitors engaged, curious, and motivated to explore different paths and possibilities on subsequent visits. It would be even better if the content can be updated, modified, or expanded over time to keep up with changing trends, technological advancements, or guest preferences. This adaptability contributes to the experience's long-term viability and relevance.

There's also the idea of creating a fanbase or a sense of loyalty among your visitors in the form of a community. Encouraging your visitors to plan meetups, return for special events, and attend regular activities fosters a sense of attachment and emotional connection to the place and experience. Create a place or a slate of programming where they immediately feel like they can play and belong.

I think of Disneybounding as an example. It's a way for Disney fans to dress up as their favorite characters using regular clothes. Guests wear similar colors, patterns, or accessories to embody the spirit of their favorite characters. There are also different types of groups that meet up in Disney parks all over the world to share and celebrate their passions. By encouraging social interaction, you enhance the overall experience and provide additional motivation for multiple visits.

Consider the games *Minecraft* and *The Legend of Zelda: Breath of the Wild*. Both are games with high replay value because they offer an expansive open-world adventure game with emergent gameplay, numerous secrets to discover, and even dynamic weather that changes the gameplay, bringing change and unpredictability that offers unique opportunities for engagement.

Here are some ways you can consider scaling playability in your experience.

Set Clear Objectives and Roles

Clearly define the objectives, roles, and responsibilities for each participant within the immersive experience. Can each participant have a unique role to play based on their skills and interests? This is a great technique to use when exploring how to meet your visitors where they are. How does a natural leader fit into the context of your world? *Who* is the leader? The second-in-command? The problem solver? The artist? The detective? The engineer? You can create opportunities in which each participant has a unique and meaningful role to play and ensure that their contributions are essential for achieving the overall goal.

Or do you flip that around and create an experience in which your visitor discovers their role in the context of your world? One of the more successful examples I've experienced is the SPYSCAPE museum in New York City. Every visitor or participant has a very

SPYSCAPE, New York City, NY. Photos by Margaret Kerrison.

clear objective: "Explore hidden worlds, break codes, run surveil-
lance and spot liars — while a system developed with MI6 experts
reveals your personal spy role and profile."[27]

---

[27] https://spyscape.com/nyc/hq

Throughout this interactive museum, you tap your RFID wristband to engage with different games, puzzles, and tests to develop your spy profile at multiple stations. At the end of the visit, your score is tallied, and a personal spy profile is created for you based on how well you did in the various mental and physical tasks scattered throughout the experience. This is a terrific example of gamifying the museum experience. One in which the visitor is invited to play and is empowered to follow their own path to create a truly unique experience with each visit.

Since my last visit, SPYSCAPE has added a new social and interactive experience with SPYGAMES: "You'll jump, climb, throw and dodge in fun immersive challenges developed with experts from CIA and Special Ops to stretch your physical and mental agility with every visit."[28] I can't wait to return and try this new experience.

An experience like SPYGAMES is a great way to encourage repeat visitation and offers a compelling invitation for participants to play together in unique ways.

Encourage Teamwork and Collaborative Gameplay

Another way to scale playability is to foster a sense of teamwork and collaboration among participants by designing challenges and puzzles that require teamwork and coordination.

As humans, we bond through play, but we also bond through shared challenges.

I mentioned earlier that Netflix offered a live-action version of the popular Korean survival drama television series *Squid Game* titled Squid Game: The Trials. They described the guest promise thus: "You've seen Squid Game on Netflix, now play it in real life. Six challenges will put your skills to the test in an immersive competition like no other. Sign up now and be one of the first to accept the Front Man's challenge. Are you ready?"[29]

---

[28] https://spyscape.com/spygames
[29] https://www.netflix.com/tudum/squid-game-the-trials

Similarly, The Void's VR experiences offered social games that encouraged collaboration between teammates. *Millennium Falcon*: Smugglers Run does the same. And escape rooms are the perfect example of collaborative gameplay. The only way to progress or successfully complete the story of the game is through player or participant collaboration. It's engaging and social. This kind of storytelling is my favorite kind of experience because it leaves the participants talking about it long after the experience ends.

Many visitors and participants are no longer interested in merely watching others partake in games; they want to partake in it themselves. Imagine going through different puzzles and challenges with the help of your teammates. Consider games that can only be accomplished successfully through effective teamwork and collaboration.

Utilize Gamemasters

This technique is especially useful when you have a large number of participants that requires a formal facilitator or gamemaster to ensure visitor enjoyment. Consider having trained gamemasters who can oversee the experience, similar to the role of the Dungeon Master in the immensely popular fantasy tabletop role-playing game *Dungeons & Dragons*, to provide assistance when needed and ensure that all players are having a fun, fulfilling time.

Squid Game had a Front Man. *The Hunger Games* had a Head Gamemaker. Consider how your experience can have a gamemaster who can orchestrate the most exciting, challenging, and fulfilling experience based on the makeup and number of participants. Perhaps the obstacles or storylines can change based on how many "players" you have in a given experience. The gamemaster ensures that the experience remains engaging and appropriately challenging regardless of the group size. They can incorporate elements that adjust difficulty, complexity, or pacing in response to player interactions. They can also offer guidance or hints to players when they are stuck, especially in larger groups when individual players might become overwhelmed. It's a great way to maintain momentum and prevent frustration.

Parallel Activities

Rather than designing an experience with a singular linear format, consider incorporating parallel activities or branching paths that accommodate multiple players pursuing different tasks simultaneously. This can prevent bottlenecks and ensure that everyone remains engaged. I imagine in the future the use of AI can help reroute and influence the crowds based on the number of participants in each location.

The parallel activities should strike a balance between competition and cooperation. Consider activities that introduce elements that encourage friendly competition among players while also requiring them to cooperate and collectively achieve overarching goals. Could they start in the same place, branch out into parallel activities, and end up in the same place to celebrate big emotional payoffs based on the actions of their activities? I think of experiences like *Sleep No More* and *Star Wars*: Galactic Starcruiser as examples of this model.

OPPORTUNITIES FOR IMMERSIVE EXPERIENCES

I wonder how museums can learn from open-world narratives and places like *Sleep No More*, in which you can explore different scenes, follow different characters, and choose your own path with each visit. Could participants immerse themselves in an important time period in history and explore the different scenes, engage with historical figures, partake in emergent activities, and choose their own paths? Imagine a place where you can explore and delve deeper into the time periods of the American Civil War, the *Titanic* voyage, or the Belle Époque with each visit.

In my experience of "*Titanic*: The Exhibition," each visitor received a unique boarding pass. Each visitor was given the name

Boarding Pass

OF

White Star Royal Mail Triple-Screw Steamer

"TITANIC"

AT BELFAST

Wednesday, 10th April, 1912, at 9.30a.m.

TO BE PRESENTED AT GATE

Titanic boarding pass. Photo by Margaret Kerrison.

and biographical information of a real passenger. At the end of the exhibit, the visitor could find their character's name on a wall to see if they survived the tragedy or not. Imagine if this exhibit became an immersive experience where visitors could return to pursue a different character or storyline, similar to the video game *Titanic: Adventure Out of Time.*

Or imagine creating your immersive experience through the perspectives of multiple characters. Developing a believable story world through the eyes of one character is challenging enough, but consider how you might create a shared story experience through multiple narrators. Imagine going through a cultural or historical moment in the perspective of all of the key players in that narrative. I'm curious about experiencing the story of any battle or war in our history through the perspective of different sides. What if we demystify and deconstruct the narrative so that it can attempt to represent all sides? Or can we go on one journey through the perspective of one side, then go on another journey through the perspective of the other side? At such experiences, participants would inhabit a different character's storyline each time they visited.

Perhaps your experience calls for a collective storytelling perspective, similar to what the 9/11 Memorial & Museum did with their emotional and engaging exhibit in New York City. "For more than a decade, StoryCorps and the 9/11 Memorial Museum have worked together on the September 11th Initiative, which aims to record one oral history to honor each life lost in the World Trade Center attacks of Sept. 11, 2001 and Feb. 26, 1993. The award-winning series preserves the stories of survivors, rescue workers, witnesses and others through audio recordings, some of which are made into animations."[30]

Imagine if you could create a historical immersive experience inspired by *Her Story*, the award-winning crime fiction game with nonlinear storytelling from Sam Barlow. The entire game revolves around a police database full of live-action video footage. Can you become an investigator, uncovering footage and other clues in the experience? Are there different unsolved historical crimes and mysteries to solve with each visit?

Or how about an immersive experience based on the game *80 Days*, a text-based adventure game in which players make decisions to navigate a journey around the world in eighty days using a variety of routes and outcomes? I can imagine there's high replay value in a space that can transport me to and immerse me in different places around the world where I can meet fellow travelers.

Replay value in immersive experiences often involves the depth of the content, interactivity, personalization, and the potential for discovering new elements with each visit. You can draw visitors back to your experience by creating the promise of engaging with new characters and storylines. You can provide unique seasonal experiences that cater to varying interests by adapting your content based on the time of the year. You can offer limited-run

---

[30] https://www.911memorial.org/connect/blog/preserving-our-history-through-storytelling

merchandise, food and beverage items, attractions, and experiences that draw in regular and new participants.

Ultimately, your experience must appeal to the constant human need to discover something new. We are accustomed to the familiar, ordinary world and are on a perpetual quest for the unfamiliar to infuse an element of surprise and awe into our existence. Never underestimate our yearning for extraordinary experiences, as they have the power to make us feel alive and truly special.

JUMP-STARTER QUESTIONS

- Who are the NPCs (nonplayable characters) in your experience, and WHY are they there?
- How will each participant engage with the others, if any others are present?
- Are there different levels to unlock? Are there rewards and achievements?
- Are there elements of collaboration or competition? If so, where and how?

CUTSCENE: AN INTERVIEW WITH AMBER SAMDAHL[31]

||||||||||||||||||||||||||||||||||||||||||||||||||||||||||||||||||||||||||||||||||||||||||||

Creative director at PBS Wisconsin, former executive creative director at Walt Disney Imagineering

MK: What did you do as part of the research and development team in your first ten years at Walt Disney Imagineering?

AS: I started off building prototypes for interactive experiences. On my first few projects, we were exploring how to integrate mobile devices and games into a theme park experience. We would be given a prompt around a technology or a spark of an idea, like — how do you seamlessly leverage wearable technology to enhance the theme park experience in the Disney Parks? Then I would work alongside a team to ideate, prototype, and playtest these experiences. We explored ways to use mobile devices, hand-held gaming devices, wearable technologies, and even social media to connect people to their families and friends and enhance the park experience.

Over time, I moved from building prototypes to focus more on creative design. I found that the through line of all of my work was connecting people through play. That led to my interest and exploration of immersive role-play experiences. In that work, we were searching for new ways to answer the question "How can guests collaborate with their family, friends, the Disney Cast Members, and other guests to create a story and experience together?"

MK: Can you tell me more about what it means to create a story as part of this team?

---

[31] This interview was conducted by Margaret Kerrison over video chat and email. The transcript has been edited for clarity and length.

AS: We started by exploring the prompt "What if we put people in the role as a character in our theme parks where they were the protagonist of their own story, and we supported them through storytelling?" The Disney Parks can do that so uniquely. We have created these rich environments and worlds, we have Cast Members and characters in our parks. What can we do with all these pieces to support the guests' stories?

What we found through early testing was that by empowering people to lead their own stories, they really enjoyed profound moments of connection, whether it was with their families, new friends they had met along the way, or the Cast Members. We were really intrigued by this idea of leveraging those connections and making that the heart of the experience.

One project that comes to mind is *The Optimist*, an alternate reality game we developed in 2013 that was based off the backstory of the *Tomorrowland* movie. The idea behind the project was to explore how we could create an alternate reality experience where a community of people all around the world, with the support of a few fictional characters, worked to unlock a story together. It was very much in the hands of the guests, whether they were in our parks, around Los Angeles, or online, all participating together to progress the story along.

MK: How did you approach that creative process?
AS: The way we developed the story and experience of *The Optimist* was very organic. We had a general narrative arc that we wanted to achieve and a list of activities that we thought would be fun and fit within the story, but it was very much a back-and-forth process between developing the story and the interactive parts of the experience. We would develop the story to a certain point, then go back to our interactions and start to pull together which activities would help progress the story forward. Then, once our interactions were more fleshed out, we would go back to the story and ask, "How is this going to piece together and move forward?"

Finding that balance is tough. There's always a scale that I'm keeping an eye on of like, "We've gone so far in the story that I'm not sure how the gameplay is going to fit in now." Or "Oh, we've gone way down the path of gameplay, are we moving away from the story?" So there's always a need to be watching both sides to see when we need to pivot back and forth. But then there's this magical flow that happens when they intersect and they weave together so seamlessly and they're in support of each other. It is a complex puzzle, but because *The Optimist* was a narrative and character-focused interactive experience, it was important to be thinking about both sides. When you find that balance, I think that's where you have the most success.

The other challenge in developing *The Optimist* was the nature of an alternate reality game. We had people playing live across multiple platforms over the course of six weeks. People were contributing and sharing ideas as it was unfolding, and we wanted to be responsive and follow their invested interests. So we made some changes on the fly by adapting the story and some of the activities based on what we were witnessing. We added elements and tweaked the ending to better fit the emotional connections people were finding with the characters. It ended up being a significantly more powerful story and experience because people were bringing their own ideas, emotions, and experiences to those stories.

MK: How do you think about engaging participants emotionally in an experience?

AS: I think *The Optimist* was such a wonderful chance to do that because we listened to the participants. They were genuinely contributing to the experience and interacting directly with the characters, so they felt heard and recognized. They were able to participate at a level that brought in their own personal selves and emotions. We had a wonderful team on the project that was very dedicated to that heartfelt storytelling, and we wanted everyone to feel that. The way we wrote the characters and how they engaged and interacted with guests was supporting that goal. It allowed people to participate in a way that told them, "We see you, we hear you." I feel like that unlocked an extra level of engagement and personal connection. I think we saved all the social media posts of people sharing their own experiences at the end of the game. The guests truly took the story and brought it into their own lives. We heard such heartwarming stories of people using the experience to build connections across generations and rekindling and mending relationships within their own families. It was incredibly emotional and powerful for all of us that shared that experience. It still gives me goose bumps to think about it!

MK: What game design techniques have you found useful in developing story-based immersive experiences?
AS: The first thing I learned at Walt Disney Imagineering is that story always comes first. So know the story you want to tell. That is the key to driving everything. The other thing that is really important and relates to games is really knowing the audience as well. It is important to remember with any interactive design, you're not creating an experience for you. You're creating experiences for other people. So first you really need to know who those other people are. What are they feeling, or what is their life experience? What are they bringing to this experience? So as you're developing the story, and then the interactive experience that weaves through it, you always have to keep that audience at the forefront of your mind.

I'd also say interactive design takes humility. You have to be able to put things out there and then be totally fine if, or more likely when, it doesn't work. You have to remember and embrace that it's not for you, it's for others. It's a very different design process than designing for more traditional storytelling experiences.

Once you have started with story, and you understand the audience, it's important to start building prototypes and start testing with your audience as soon as possible. These can be simple prototypes that help move your interactive design forward. Every opportunity you have to playtest gives you more information to understand your audience so that your experience gets better. So early and frequent testing with prototypes and then continuing to iterate.

MK: How do you think about designing an experience that can be enjoyed by most, if not all, participants?

AS: Yeah, that's a really hard challenge. Designing for a broad audience. I think one of the best techniques to approach that is through playtesting to get to know your audience. That means being there in person, if possible, and observing them. And then asking questions and really actively listening to understand what they are experiencing. You don't want to project your own thoughts or ideas. You have to be very good at listening and empathizing with what they're feeling. There's definitely a technique to making sure people feel comfortable sharing, especially in early prototypes of experiences when the work is still really rough.

Sometimes we will see a guest testing something, and if it's just not working, we will have to reassure them. We will tell them that it's not their fault. That it's our fault. We explain that we haven't designed it well enough yet, and that's why it's so important they're here to help us understand what's not working so we can make it better. People might be nervous or don't want to be embarrassed, right? Sometimes they'll just quickly shut down or blame themselves as a protection measure. "Oh, I don't play games. I'm sure it's just me." It's completely understandable why people might feel that way, but we get the best-quality information when we can make people feel comfortable and get at the heart of what they're experiencing. As designers, we need to say "You are doing great. You are exactly who we want. Your voice is important." Because if we can unlock those voices and better understand what's not working for them, we can improve the experience for everyone — so that more and more people *can* be successful. It's so important that everyone's voices are included in that. And that all goes back to humility and empathy, two of the key qualities that I truly believe make the best interactive designers.

Another important part of the process is to playtest with as many different people as you can. Every demographic you can, in different situations, trying to best simulate the final audience and experience. It can be really challenging to recruit and engage with that wide variety of demographics, but it is so important to build that into the process.

MK: How do you personally measure the success of your projects?

AS: That is a good question. It probably depends on the project. *The Optimist* didn't have a long lifespan, or a huge reach because of that short lifespan, but it is a project that I continue to be extremely proud of. And I think the whole team that worked on it feels the same way because of the impact it had. It was emotionally powerful and meaningful to so many of us. There are players that still have a community and connect based on their shared foundation through that game. For me, witnessing the emotional comments and conversations that happened throughout the experience, and that depth of engagement — that is what made it a success.

More broadly for me, success is when we have created an experience that inspires people to try something new. When people are comfortable to let their guard down a bit and engage and play wholeheartedly. I think it's that playful mindset that really opens people up to new experiences and to each other. Play has such a power to build connections and strengthen bonds between people. And I think that is the ultimate measure of success.

*"Research is formalized curiosity. It is poking
and prying with a purpose."*

— Zora Neale Hurston, anthropologist and author

9

BUT HOW DO YOU DO IT?

I CAN'T COUNT THE NUMBER OF times people ask me "How do you actually do it? Can you give us step-by-step instructions on how to create an immersive experience?"

Unfortunately, creating an engaging and meaningful experience doesn't come with an instructional guide. I know many of you *want* a practical guide, but here's the honest truth: There isn't one. There are frameworks you can use, and I've provided some jump-starter questions at the end of each chapter and collected in Appendix A, but ultimately, you need to find your own process. Why? Because creating your experience depends on many important factors.

Creating an immersive experience depends on your target audience, your client, your IP and story, the location of your experience, the stakeholders, your budget and schedule, your team makeup, your organization or company, and the way your individual mind works as a designer. There isn't a one-size-fits-all solution to creating an immersive experience. If anyone tries to tout a magic formula to creating your immersive experience, you should be skeptical. It doesn't exist.

This industry is about researching, listening, receiving feedback, iterating, and continually changing based on the needs and desires of all of the stakeholders involved in your project. It also involves being innovative and trying different ways that you never considered previously. It's about drawing insights and lessons from different fields and industries so that you can innovate within your own.

There isn't any "one way" to design an experience for a museum. There isn't any "one way" to design for a theme park ride. Every project I've worked on has been a different journey.

My advice is to start with curiosity. Start by listening, learning, and researching. Always ask "Why does it have to be this way?" Question the story, the medium, and the guest experience. Think about what will be meaningful and engaging for your audience. Home in on their wish fulfillment and how it manifests in the experience. Think about combining different perspectives, methods, mediums, and participant actions. But remember they must all serve the meaning and the context of the experience.

Every individual has a different creative process, which means that every team and every company will need to find and set a process that works for them. Ultimately, everyone needs to understand and align with how they're going to work together so that they can all be pieces of the puzzle building toward the same big picture. How you work together will tremendously affect your product. Believe me, it will be evident to your participant.

With that said, if I can give you a practical step-by-step framework, this is what I can provide:

1. DEFINE YOUR GOAL OR OBJECTIVE

Clearly identify and define the purpose of your immersive experience. Is it to entertain, educate, inform, enlighten, inspire, or do something else? What's your mission statement? It could be a thought-provoking question, a problem to solve, a bold statement, or a compelling call to action for the visitor.

2. KNOW YOUR AUDIENCE

Research your target audience's preferences, interests, and expectations. Tailor your experience to resonate with them. Do you have secondary audiences? Who are they? The goal is to capture your audience's attention, spark their interest, and leave them eager to learn more. Begin with a captivating guest promise to grab the audience's attention immediately. You'll be surprised by how many pitches I've seen that don't start with a strong hook or guest promise. Furthermore, many creatives don't seem to have conviction in their ideas. If you, as the creator, lack conviction, how do you expect other people to buy into your idea?

3. FIND THE BIG IDEA

Brainstorm ideas that align with your objective and audience. Consider themes, narratives, and interactive elements that will enhance engagement. Ask the big storytelling questions of Why, What, When, Where, Who, and How. Convey the emotional impact or transformative potential of the immersive experience. Explain how participants will feel or what they will gain from engaging with the experience from the start, during, and at the end of the experience. Highlight the emotional takeaway visitors can expect from participating in the immersive experience. Whether it's personal growth, new skills, unique perspectives, or lasting memories, emphasize the value they will receive.

4. CRAFT A COMPELLING CONCEPT

Craft a narrative that drives the experience. What is the narrative thrust — the driving force behind a story's progression and the element that compels your participant to continue engaging with the narrative? It should be relatable, engaging, and emotionally resonant. Highlight what makes it unique, innovative, or intriguing. Use evocative language to paint a vivid mental picture. Use visual aids, images, mood boards, and graphics to communicate your concept. Be clear, concise, and compelling.

Briefly outline how participants will be engaged and involved in the experience in a way that involves more than just being passive observers. Highlight any interactive elements, role-playing, or activities that will immerse them fully. Make sure that all of the activities aren't random or isolated from one another. They should be aligned and interconnected to tell the same story in the same world and in the same context. They should all speak to the same theme.

I always use this analogy: If I take any member of your team and interrogate them in separate rooms, they should all tell the same story. If they're not telling the same story, then there's a problem with the project's vision and alignment.

5. CHOOSE THE CORRECT MEDIUM

Determine whether your immersive experience is better expressed in digital form (traditional media, VR, augmented reality, video game, etc.) or physical form (theme park, museum exhibit, escape room, interactive exhibit, exploratory setting). What is the best way to communicate your narrative to engage your participants? Why does it need to be in person or in a physical environment? There has to be a strong reason WHY. You shouldn't create a physical space filled with multiple screens and call it "immersive."

6. DESIGN THE ENVIRONMENT

Create the physical or virtual space where the experience will take place. Pay attention to every detail: the aesthetics, lighting, sound, and overall ambiance. If using media and technology, make sure they are seamlessly integrated and enhance the immersion rather than distracting from it. Incorporate sound effects, music, visuals, props, characters, and other storytelling techniques to evoke emotions. Consider ways to engage multiple senses, such as touch, smell, and taste, if appropriate.

7. BUILD OUT THE GAMEPLAY AND GUEST FLOW

Identify how participants will engage with the experience. Consider the first-person perspective — their feelings and actions. Will they solve puzzles, make decisions, or interact with characters? Map out the participant's journey from start to finish. Walk in their shoes. Define how they will progress through different stages of the experience and how they will feel. How will they be transformed by the end of the experience? What will be their emotional takeaway? Explore options for the duration, logistics, and any other details that are relevant, such as location, accessibility, or dates.

8. PLAYTEST AND REFINE

Invite trusted partners and colleagues. Pilot the experience with a small group to gather feedback. Use this feedback to refine and improve the experience. Test again. Refine again.

9. TRAIN AND STAFF

If your immersive experience involves human interaction, train your staff to ensure they understand the narrative and can enhance your participants' immersion and engagement. Can they bring their own personal stories and experiences into your narrative, as long as they're aligned with the context of your narrative?

10. MAKE YOUR GUEST PROMISE

Truthfully and effectively market your immersive experience, clearly conveying what participants can expect. What's the wish fulfillment? Build anticipation and set expectations with a compelling guest promise.

11. COLLECT FEEDBACK

After participants go through the experience, gather feedback to further refine and enhance future iterations. Even after the initial launch, continue to monitor and improve the experience based on feedback and changing audience expectations. Keep learning, iterating, and evolving.

Besides the steps I've outlined, I've also included at the end of this book some tools that you can use in the form of the Jump-Starter Questions, Previsualization Storytelling Tools, and Considerations for Creating an Engaging Guest Journey. Remember that creating an immersive experience requires a blend of art, creativity, storytelling, technology, humanity, and attention to detail. Collaborate with trusted thought partners and a diverse team to bring different perspectives and expertise to the process, and be willing to adapt and iterate based on feedback and real-world testing.

"It's much more like the theater in a way, where the creatives gather and a narrative emerges. We start with the story in the center, and then begin to process the story . . . a kind of framing for how multiple narratives can spring out of one world space, and how the opportunities might [achieve] a new kind of storytelling."

— ALEX McDOWELL, NARRATIVE DESIGNER AND
WORLD BUILDER

10

BREAKING INTO IMMERSIVE EXPERIENCES

ERE'S THE TRUTH. I fell into this line of work based on the convergence of my curiosities: writing, storytelling, content development, creative strategy, sociology, psychology, narrative placemaking, brand positioning, environmental design, urban planning, architecture, social design, and experiential design. I went from designing museums, brand centers, and world expos to writing for indie films, educational series, and children's animation to designing theme parks and immersive experiences.

There is no perfect job role that encompasses everything that I do. When I need to describe what I do, I come up with titles like Immersive Storyteller or Narrative Lead. Ultimately, I'm a champion of narrative. A guardian of story. But it's more than just championing and guarding. It's building a set of values and designing a framework that is driven by narrative, which will hold the entire work together. It's this commitment to aligning, defining, iterating, and refining the narrative of the work. I find meaning for the project and the people that it serves.

Immersive experiences are tools for any industry to use to their advantage. They're a way for organizations and companies to create meaningful engagement with their customers or fanbase. Unfortunately, other industries still have a lot to learn from the gaming industry, which understands the value of a narrative director on every creative endeavor. While projects related to themed entertainment or immersive experiences typically feature a creative director and an art director, the absence of a narrative director is problematic. This gap is well-addressed in the gaming realm, where a dedicated creative director oversees the overarching creative direction of a game, the art director handles visual and design aspects, and the narrative director caters to the player experience. This comprehensive approach highlights the importance of integrating narrative directors into the teams of various industries, especially those seeking to engage participants, guests, visitors, audience members, or users in their real-world encounters.

You may occasionally find writing positions open, and when you do, you should apply. Get your foot in the door. It's not easy and the job is highly competitive, but there's never any harm in trying. I started at Walt Disney Imagineering as a consultant, then a show writer, and then ended up becoming managing story editor and de facto story and narrative lead for the *Star Wars* portfolio for many years.

When you apply for a writing job for an immersive experience or theme park company, be prepared to share your best work. Typically, they ask for writing samples that come in different formats. They may ask to read a sample of writing that describes a place or environment to demonstrate your ability to write descriptively for a guest journey, a script that demonstrates your ability to write characters and dialogue, and perhaps other written materials such as copywriting or marketing materials.

What are companies looking for in writing samples? The same principles for screenwriting in film, TV, and games apply to immersive experiences. In the first few pages, you want to hook your audience. You don't have time to waste. Reveal character depth, advance the plot, and immerse your participants in the story within the first couple of minutes. Give them a sense of the world and quickly demonstrate the hierarchy and dynamics of the characters' relationships with one another. Build your world. Make me believe in it. Make me want to know more.

As a hiring manager, I can immediately get a sense of a writer's ability in the first two pages. Good writers make their story "sing." They paint a vivid picture of the world, demonstrate a strong POV, introduce the characters and story in a unique way, and, most importantly, get to the point. You're not writing a novel, you're writing an experience. Every scene should serve a purpose. In designing immersive experiences, you may not always have a linear storytelling medium (i.e., traditional media) to tell your story, but consider how parts of the experience can communicate the story, similar to how games display cutscenes to develop a character or progress the story forward.

In the School of Cinematic Arts at USC, I learned that a great scene accomplishes at least one of three things: It sets the mood and world, it adds to a character's development or relationship with another character, or it progresses the plot. Share writing examples that demonstrate how you envision each scene of your experience accomplishing at least one of these three things. Even better if you can accomplish all three in one scene.

When I think of a "scene" in an immersive experience, it's the physical space in which a world, character, or story element is revealed. Consider Disney's Pirates of the Caribbean ride. Each scene is a different space in which the next part of the story is revealed. It's like one big immersive storyboard. In addition to the environmental storytelling, the dialogue between the characters (the audio-animatronics) also helps to reveal the story of the world.

If you also have skills as an artist, illustrator, graphic designer, producer, researcher, creative director, even better. Companies are always looking for multitalented people who can bring in different perspectives to their work. Demonstrate how you're a fast learner and can hit the ground running. Be a team player, be collaborative, and be professional. *Always* be professional. Be curious, be open to other fields and industries, be a forever student, ask questions, and don't be afraid to say "I don't know."

JUMP-STARTER QUESTIONS

- What industries, topics, or stories do you care about deeply? What new immersive experiences can you envision for these interests?

CUTSCENE:
AN INTERVIEW WITH
MARGARET KERRISON

||||||||||||||||||||||||||||||||||||||||||||||||||||||||||||||||||||||||||||||||||||||||||||||||||||

Author, immersive storyteller, and narrative lead

This interview first appeared in *Exhibition* (Fall 2023) vol. 42, no. 2, and is reproduced with permission from the American Alliance of Museums (AAM).[32]

MARGARET CHANDRA KERRISON:
ON STORYTELLING, NARRATIVE PLACEMAKING,
AND PUSHING BOUNDARIES

In this issue, editor Jeanne Normand Goswami interviews Margaret Chandra Kerrison, former Walt Disney Imagineer and author of *Immersive Storytelling for Real and Imagined Worlds: A Writer's Guide* (Michael Wiese Productions, 2022), to learn more about the importance of story to placemaking, the potential of immersive spaces to build connection, and what she's working on next.

Q Jeanne: It's great to meet you, Margaret. Could you begin by telling our readers a bit about your career path?
A Margaret: I've always been a writer, ever since I could hold a pencil. It has always been a very big part of me, but I never really considered it as a career. I moved to the United States when I was eighteen, and when I graduated from college, I happened to take a screenwriting course and absolutely fell in love with this whole format of writing and telling stories.

When my husband and I moved to L.A. eighteen years ago, he went to USC for public policy, and I got my master's in screenwriting. But coming out of that program, it felt very limiting to just tell

---

[32] This interview was conducted by Jeanne Normand Goswami over video chat. The transcript has been lightly edited for clarity and length: www.aam-us.org/programs/exhibition-journal/

stories on the screen because that's not how I told stories in my mind. One of my thesis professors mentioned that all kinds of industries need writers — everything from film to TV to video games; even rollercoasters need writers. That night I looked it up, and I found this whole world of themed entertainment. I immediately cold emailed a bunch of companies to say, I'm graduating from film school. I don't have any experience in this, but I'd love to learn.

And one of the companies that replied was BRC Imagination Arts. The founder of the company, Bob Rogers, was a writer and a storyteller himself; he had worked at Disney and directed his own films. So, he appreciated the art of storytelling. And when I went into that industry, it was mostly to do museum and brand design work. I worked with BRC on the Heineken Experience and the NASA Kennedy Space Center Visitor Complex. BRC opened my eyes to this other world of storytelling and world building and immersion that you cannot get through just the screen — being able to feel a story with all your senses and to have a role to play in the experience, to have agency to influence your environment.

I love the idea of having agency in a story or experience. Can you say a bit more about the role it plays in your work?
A: The idea that you could influence the story you're in was very intriguing and exciting for me. I grew up as a gamer. I played a lot of Nintendo, and that was something that felt very empowering as a child: to be able to have this very direct effect on your environment and to play an important role in this bigger story. Museums, theme parks, and other experiences that recognize this desire, that can tap into it, and grant that wish fulfillment, are the ones that are going to capture their visitors' hearts, minds, and imaginations.

The other thing that drives me as a storyteller is embracing the fact that every single person who walks into an experience is from a different background and comes from a different state of mind. How do you build an experience that is inviting and welcoming to all, that feels like a place where people can not only belong, but have the invitation to play, and to engage, and to connect with each other in a very safe and inviting and compelling way? Because, ultimately, every single experience that I work on, I want everyone to walk in, experience something meaningful together, and walk out believing that they're stepping into a better world. I want their mindsets and perspectives to have changed for the better, so that they feel hopeful and optimistic and question why things are the way they are. Why are certain stories being told, and who is telling them? We need to question all that.

How do you define "immersive experience" for yourself and for the teams you work with?
A: An immersive experience is many things, but the most successful ones all involve certain elements:

1. They're multisensory: you can use all your senses, not just your eyes or ears.
2. They're dynamic and adaptive: nothing is static in terms of content or presentation.
3. They're social: we have the chance to connect with one another and with ourselves to really understand the greater meaning of whatever topic is being presented.
4. They suspend my disbelief: I believe that I'm in this place, so that everything else falls away, and I can fully immerse myself in this new world.
5. They give me agency: the place itself acknowledges that I'm part of the story, and that, even if it's a minor role that I play, it's a role, nonetheless.

Are there any immersive experiences that you've visited recently which you've found particularly successful?
A: teamLab Planets in Tokyo just took my breath away. Not only was the art itself extremely beautiful and engaging, but there was a lot of surprise and delight, and discovery and exploration, and using your entire body to experience a place. When you line up,

they do a little preshow of what to expect; some of the rules. And immediately, it tells you that you can bring your cell phone if you want to take pictures, but you'll have to take off your socks and shoes. And I remember, I was with my family, and they were like, No, no, no. I'm backing out. Nope, not taking off my socks and shoes. And I'm like, just accept it, and let it go. Just go on this journey, because how often do we get to do that? So, we went into this locker room, and we put our socks and shoes away. And one of the first things we did was climb a waterfall.

Immediately, you're taken into a different place. One moment you're in bustling Tokyo, and then you go into this experience, and suddenly, the mood and the tone and the emotion of the place is just so beautiful and relaxing. Yet you're also being very social and connected. And it is very dynamic and adaptive: you have art that interacts with you that you can push and pull and touch and feel and grab, and water is dripping from your fingers. I didn't think about anything else, except being in that experience, in that moment, with the people that I love. It was a magical way for us to discover a new place together. The fact that everyone in our group from my nine-year-old son to my forty-eight-year-old brother loved it so much speaks to how wonderful that experience was.

Another really shining example for me is the Smithsonian's National Museum of African American History and Culture (NMAAHC) in Washington, DC.

I don't even see it as a museum; I see it as an experience. The architecture of the building is astounding. And then you start your experience in this dim basement, in the bowels of a slave ship — immediately, bang, emotionally, you know that this is not going to be an easy experience. And yet, the museum takes you on that journey and makes you feel like you're really getting a sense of walking in someone else's shoes, in a different place and time. You are immersed in that history in a way that feels very important and very emotionally compelling. And then you literally, physically, move up through the floors of the museum to the light, to the very top, where all this natural light is coming in, and experience that journey from slavery to celebration, and you feel it in your body as you move.

And the thing about that experience, too, is that it made me feel connected. I was having conversations with other visitors in a way that I've never experienced before in a museum. People I didn't know were chatting with me and sharing their thoughts. I wasn't asking questions; we were just looking at the same thing and would strike up a conversation about really challenging things. And that's extremely moving because it's not something that we can easily do in our daily lives. And that's why, for me, one of the most important elements of any immersive experience is that it has to be social. It needs to connect you to a larger whole.

What strikes me in these examples is the way teamLab and NMAAHC have built spaces that feel distinct from the world that surrounds them. They've created these sanctuaries that give people the freedom to think, react, and interact differently, and this allows the experience to resonate in deep and lasting ways. How in your work as a storyteller do you help to shape these types of spaces?

A: What's most important as a team is to really think about why you're building this place. All of you are coming from different backgrounds, and you're also carrying your own unconscious biases and assumptions and opinions on what this topic is about. So, to come together as a team and be aligned with why this is important, why you're telling this story, why you're building this place, and who it's for is absolutely essential before you start talking about how it's going to look and what people are going to do there.

As a team, you must align your creative intent. And, frequently, by asking these questions, you realize you don't agree. The fact that there are contradictory opinions on your small team is very telling about how the topic will be received by the public. So, you really need to allow time for exploration, research, and dialogue — not only within your teams, but also with those outside. You need to ask: Who do we need to bring in to expand this conversation? Who will challenge us to see past our own biases and thinking? How can we expand upon this topic to be as thorough and authentic as possible?

Once you've had those conversations, you can begin to collectively identify the value system that will guide your group throughout the design process. And because you have that shared value system, then you can move forward in a way that's not, we want to do it because it looks cool. Or, we want to do it because kids will like it. Instead, you're asking: Does it fit into our guiding principles and values? Because if it doesn't, it doesn't belong there.

Have you ever been part of a team where you haven't been able to find that common ground?
A: All the time. The process that I outline in my book is one in which everything falls in order. First, we do this, then this, then this. But it almost never happens that way. I've been pulled into projects where they've already started designing, and then they bring me in and say, We've got story problems; help us fix them. Those are the most challenging projects to be in because I wasn't part of that journey from the beginning. And, as a team, you need to have that shared context and history to understand why decisions were made. I find that projects are most successful when a writer or a storyteller is in it from day one, so they're able to help guide conversations and be the wrangler of what's important and what's not.

How would you approach professionals who are used to storytelling in one setting or medium to encourage them to think in broader terms about how we tell stories for humans, wherever they may be, in ways that make them feel like a particular experience is speaking directly to them?
A: People today don't differentiate, or compartmentalize, how or where they experience story. I just look at my son and the way

he easily toggles between his physical and digital worlds, without thinking this is a story that I'm experiencing in real life, versus at a theme park, versus on my Nintendo Switch or phone or iPad. He's just there, enjoying the experience and immersed in the story, without regard for the vessel or container of it.

We are spoiled for choice. We can experience stories in every medium, all around us. Whether we want to sit on our couch and binge a Netflix series or get up and go into a museum or to a concert, we have so many choices and a lot more leisure time. So, ultimately, no matter what industry you're in — theme park, museum, video, gaming, film, TV — you need to have a growth mindset. You need to ask, What other ways can we be innovative?

We're always looking for something unique, compelling, and emotionally resonant. The more that an industry resists change or feels like its stories or experiences shouldn't change, then it and its audiences lose out, because people are not static. Life is not static. We're always changing. We're always moving. We're always growing. So, we need our institutions to believe in that, too, and to be able to adapt and grow with the community and with the culture.

When I join projects, my favorite question to ask is, Why should I care? Why is this important? Why am I doing this rather than something else? The more museums and cultural institutions can authentically answer that question, the more they'll be moving in the right direction.

What drives you in your creative practice? How do you keep pushing the boundaries of storytelling?
A: I've learned something from each of my projects. And for each one of them, there's something different that I'm proud of. It's interesting because I came from museum design and brand visitor design, not having any experience in it, and I went to theme park design at Imagineering with zero theme park experience. And so, for me, I'm always chasing my curiosity. I'm always trying to fulfill this need to learn and grow and ask questions: Why can't we do

it that way? What if we did it this way? Why not? That outsider's mindset has allowed me to see other ways of approaching things.

I always believe that my best project is yet to come. This optimistic mindset is a constant in my work. As is my relentless pursuit of trying to find new ways to tell stories, of improving upon projects that I've worked on before. I never want to do the same thing twice; it kills me as a creative. I always want to push the boundaries and see what I can get away with. It's kind of my MO. And I'm inspired by companies and people that do that, too.

What's next on the horizon for you?
A: I'm working on a second book [*Reimagined Worlds: Narrative Placemaking for People, Play, and Purpose*] that I describe as a designer's manifesto to build a more people-centric, narrative-driven world. It's an exploration of how some built environments and experiences have completely changed the way we think about things by asking those what-if and why-not questions. Cirque du Soleil, for example. They asked, Can you build a circus without animals? And look at what they've done. Absolutely mind-blowing, amazing work.

What's a theme park without rides? That's what Meow Wolf has done. What's an art museum where you can touch everything? That's what teamLab has done and Meow Wolf, too. So, when you ask these questions, and when you break that mold of what you think you are, or who you think you should be, that's when you find this gold that's been sitting there all along. Because it's never too late for anyone to reinvent and to reimagine themselves.

As people, we want to be pushed and challenged in new and creative ways. So, how can you, the creator and storyteller, make that space for us? How can you give us those opportunities to be creative, to be compassionate, and to socialize and have that sense of community and connection with people? How can you blow up the idea of what something should or shouldn't be by not being afraid to ask what if and why not?

*"Tell me what you pay attention to and
I will tell you who you are."*

— José Ortega y Gasset, philosopher and essayist

11

THE CASE FOR IRL
(IN REAL LIFE) EXPERIENCES

I LOVE PLAYING VIDEO GAMES. So much so that it has influenced me as a writer and storyteller to write this book of valuable insights and lessons. I continually take the lessons that I learn from playing video games into everything that I do as a creative. With that said, I still value physical, in-person experiences. I would rather go to a physical experience rather than a virtual one. We need more compelling IRL experiences. Now more than ever.

In a world where we're addicted to our screens, where we would rather socialize online than in-person, and where we choose to work, sleep, play, and socialize from the comforts of our homes, we need to unplug, go places, meet people, and use all of our senses again. We need to feel each other's presence, read each other's verbal and nonverbal cues, and learn to connect with others again.

I'd love to find more ways to play with family, friends, and strangers IRL. We don't make enough time to play by ourselves, let alone with one another. I'm always looking for new and interesting ways to play and engage. How can we look up from our screens and meaningfully engage with each other? How can we be in the moment and feel alive?

As I wrote in my second book, *Reimagined Worlds,*

> Human beings are social animals and need social interaction to thrive. It's what we're wired to do and how we understand our role in society. Spending time with others can help us feel connected and reduce feelings of

loneliness and isolation. We want to feel needed; to be a part of something bigger than ourselves. When we feel like we're an important part of a symbiotic relationship with our community members, we feel seen, heard, and most importantly, valued. We need to be in shared places with other people so we can be at leisure with one another.[33]

With rapid improvements in technology, most of the things we used to do we no longer *have* to do (calling someone on the phone, watching movies in theaters, exercising in gyms, shopping in malls). On the flip side, with rapid improvements in technology, we don't know what to do with our free time anymore, except to go right back to technology (streaming shows, playing video games, doomscrolling). It has come to the point where we have to make a conscious effort to put down our phones or turn away from our screens and go out of our homes. What was once something we used to look forward to doing (e.g., going to movie theaters with friends, going to an office or campus, socializing) now requires more work.

When you walk around in the real world, there is no manual to interpret what we are experiencing. We have to interpret it for ourselves. That takes a lot of cognitive effort, which "refers to the amount of thinking and interpretation required in order to decipher verbal information (Van Trijp 2016). Westbrook and Braver (2015) equated cognitive effort with 'effort-based decision-making' on the auditory information received in class for effective meaning-making."[34]

When we walk down a street and pass the coffee shop, located right next to the busy laundromat, next to the taco shop, the tattoo parlor, and the group of kids hanging outside the convenience store, there is a dissonance. We are constantly bombarded

[33] Margaret Kerrison, *Reimagined Worlds: Narrative Placemaking for People, Play, and Purpose.*

[34] Blumenthal and Sefotho, "Effects of Cognitive Effort," https://www.ncbi.nlm.nih.gov/pmc/articles/PMC9634669/

and distracted with disharmonious or mismatched elements. Why do you think you get so exhausted from walking through a mall? Besides fighting the crowds, you're also receiving a sensory overload of competing visual and audio cues in the forms of ads, brands, merchandise, and music blasting from stores. It's hard for your mind to quickly make sense of things and feel at ease.

Every time you play a new game or enter a new kind of physical immersive experience venue like Meow Wolf, you feel like a child again. You learn new meanings and relationships between people and objects that carry a different set of values from the real world. The same rules don't apply in a Meow Wolf world as in the real world. In the real world, you don't find yourself entering a new dimension when you go into your washing machine. That's what makes Meow Wolf appealing for many visitors: the novelty of shifting your perspective of the world. Or to simply go back in time and experience being a child again.

I make these points because 1) as experience designers, we have to make our places and experiences compelling and meaningful enough for people (especially younger generations) to feel convinced that it is worth visiting in real life with other people, and 2) we have the responsibility to create more places for community, connection, and belonging because many of these places are increasingly becoming obsolete. Our former "third places" — a term coined by sociologist Ray Oldenburg referring to those places where people spend time between home (the "first" place) and work (the "second" place) — such as college campuses, offices, churches, gyms, social clubs, cafés, and libraries — are becoming less important in the social fabric of our lives. So what are we doing to replace them?

We must continue to create places, experiences, and worlds where we encourage people to come together and create a community based on their shared interests. We have to build places that put the participant first and give them the opportunity to feel like they're a part of something bigger than themselves.

When you design something for others to experience, you share your perspective and insights into what your story is about. This is the difference between an artist and a designer. You are not creating something for design's sake, you are designing something for a future participant, player, or user. As a designer, you have an end user. You have a clear objective. Whether you're designing a game, website, restaurant, or hotel, you are designing with the intent that a participant, player, or user is going to experience your work.

How you differentiate yourself from other creators and storytellers is to clearly and concisely share your unique perspective in the context of your world. When your participant/audience member comes to your experience, they subconsciously want to know:

What do YOU think?

They want to know what you, as the designer, think about the story and the world. Consider some of your favorite storytellers, whether they are authors, filmmakers, screenwriters, game designers, architects, or another type of storyteller. They have a strong point of view. They tell you exactly what they think of their story and designed space.

In experiencing your design world, you should give participants clear prompts, rules, and suggestions on what role they should play, what they should do, and how they fit into the greater whole. Your participants absolutely want to find meaning in your experience, because they want to find meaning in their own lives. It's how they will make sense of what they encounter and how they will feel transformed coming out of your experience. They will walk away with a clear call to action, feeling that they have a greater purpose to fulfill, inspired by the role they just played in your experience and immersed in the beautiful story world that you've created for them. You have given them the wonderful opportunity to imagine what's possible and feel like an important character with a role to play using their power of agency. If you are successful as a designer, then your participants will be inspired to take action in their regular lives.

Use your superpower. Use the power of narrative to drive connection between people. The hope is that when you care and create a meaningful narrative full of positive intention, then your visitor will walk away feeling like they care too, they will be changed by it, and your experience will lead them to action. Were they so moved and inspired that they want to take action in their everyday lives?

Designing a strong narrative gives meaning to our world and to ourselves, shining a light on the connections we share with one another. It involves shifting our mindset to not only designing something magical and memorable, but also something meaningful long after the experience ends.

As Joseph Campbell said, "A hero is someone who has given his or her life to something bigger than oneself." How do we create places and experiences where every person can feel like the hero of their own story?

Let's build those places, so they will come.

JUMP-STARTER QUESTIONS

- What new understanding and questions about their own world do you hope your visitors take away from your experience?

CUTSCENE: AN INTERVIEW WITH BRUCE VAUGHN[35]

|||||||||||||||||||||||||||||||||||||||||||||||||||||||||||||||||||||||||||||||||

Chief Creative Officer of Walt Disney Imagineering

MK: What makes an immersive experience truly engaging for an audience?

BV: An engaging immersive experience requires several key elements:

1. **Safety and Reassurance:** At Imagineering, we design immersive experiences with the intention of evoking very specific emotions, and we want to bring out the child in adults so they can have a truly shared experience with their friends and family. The emotions we look to evoke are happiness, joy, and a sense that magical things can happen around them. To achieve this, we need to create environments that offer a sense of safety and reassurance. The safety aspect is critical for obvious reasons. Perhaps more impactful, though, is the sense of reassurance. Reassurance goes beyond safety in that one can feel safe, as in "I don't feel threatened," but not necessarily reassured. For instance, you can feel safe standing close to a railing on top of a very tall building, but you may still feel uneasy. Reassurance is a state in which one can let go of fear and inhibitions.

2. **Suspension of Disbelief:** Successful immersive experiences allow participants to suspend disbelief and become fully absorbed in the environment. Often, this involves creating credible illusions and maintaining a high level of quality and detail, similar to the work of a magician. At some point during a magic act, if

---

[35] This interview was conducted by Margaret Kerrison over video chat and email. The transcript has been edited for clarity and length.

successful, the audience will stop analyzing how a trick is done and just surrender to the idea that maybe magic is real. In this way, we use perception as a tool in creating a satisfying immersive experience. For example, in Autopia, our job as Imagineers wasn't to give kids the ability to actually drive a car. Not many responsible adults would willingly climb into a car that a young child is driving. Rather, our job was to make the kids BELIEVE they're driving a car. In this case, perception truly is reality, and the wish of the child is fulfilled safely.

3. Emotional Connection: Strong emotional responses are evoked through carefully designed elements that resonate with the audience on a personal level. This could be through relatable characters, compelling stories, or sensory triggers. Our guests generally arrive at our parks with the emotional connections to favorite characters and places already installed through long-form media. It's our job to home in on the key elements and details that will trigger those emotions. For instance, the shape and color language of a place, like a castle. Or the color of a character's hair combined with a specific dress. Add an iconic song associated with that place and character, and our guests feel the way they felt when they fell in love with that character's story the first time. But this time, the guest is there in the story!

4. Sharing with Others: We all enjoy sharing our favorite places and moments with loved ones. Through conscious design, we create opportunities for our guests to share something that has deep emotional, and often nostalgic, value to them with their family and friends. The key is not only maintaining the elements that created the original feeling, but to thoughtfully evolve the experience over time so it maintains a sense of the original without becoming dated. This allows multigenerations to return time and again and share a precious moment together.

5. Interactivity and Agency: Giving participants a sense of control and the ability to influence their experience is tricky in the context of a theme park. Our parks are designed primarily for shared experiences, with a focus on bringing friends and families closer together. Sometimes agency is desired, but unlike in a game, our focus needs to be as much on the interaction between the guests as the environment. For this reason, the kinds of interactivity that work best in our parks are typically unique spins on familiar group activities. For instance, scoring points in a midway game themed to *Toy Story*. We also usually only have a few minutes to deliver a satisfying interactive experience, unlike in a game one can play for hours. The essential thing is to reinforce the guest's action with a reaction in the environment. They need to know their actions cause immediate physical consequences.

6. Multisensory Engagement: One of the most exciting aspects of physical experience design is we can use all the senses to immerse a guest. By engaging multiple senses (sight, sound, smell, touch, taste), I believe the experience is more impactful, and the opportunity for suspension of disbelief is greater. Observing someone doing something may build anticipation to do that thing yourself, but it doesn't create the same memory as actually having done it. Environmental sound, smell, and texture are very powerful design elements to leverage in immersive experiences. They often trigger memories, which in turn evoke emotions.

7. Familiarity and Discovery: Layered details and intricate design allow for repeat visits and new discoveries, keeping the experience fresh and exciting each time. It's a balance of designing for consistency and familiarity so that guests can repeatedly experience something that has emotional value to them, but you must also give them the opportunity to uncover more layers with each visit. As designers, we must always have space for a bit of mystery and magic. Consider the core elements to your story that have enough familiarity but still allow for discovery. I find it's useful to distill those core elements through the eyes of a child, meaning either observe how a child reacts to something in the real world or remember how something made you feel when you were very young. People from around the world tend to react to things in a more common way when children. Those reactions tend to differ more as we become adults. When designing for groups, often multigenerational, finding those common threads is gold.

8. Feeling Successful: A great advantage of an interactive experience is the opportunity to make people feel successful. At Dreamscape Immersive, where our guests are in groups of four in an untethered, virtual-reality world, we wanted to allow them a lot of agency. At the same time, we wanted them all to feel successful at the end of the twelve-minute experience. There is no success without failure, or, more importantly, the perception there could be failure. In a longer experience, where a player can fail and get back up to try again, failures are more common than successes. In those cases, mastery is the goal of the experience. In shorter form experiences, more sleight of hand in design is needed to create a sense one might fail, but success is almost always delivered. I say "almost" because there are experiences in which failure can be nearly as fun as success. Escape rooms are one example that comes to mind. Some folks may return to solve the game, but due to the "frantic group scrambling to beat the clock" nature of many escape rooms, it's more about the journey than the destination. Either way, fun and a desire to return, even if to fail again, are important design goals.

MK: How do you measure the success of an immersive experience?

BV: How well does the experience evoke the emotion you want your guest to feel? Disney is interested in evoking specific emotions, such as a sense of joy, happiness, curiosity, and discovery. Audiences develop emotional connections with their favorite stories and characters in long-form media like movies and streaming series. When they go to real-life experiences, they're looking to feel those same emotions, but in a new way . . . in a physical environment. If you don't have a particular IP to work with, then you can use genres. Walt Disney used genres to define the lands of

Disneyland. George Lucas created *Star Wars* based on the Western genre, combined with the hero's journey. The genre becomes the familiar "place" a new story can live in. Space Mountain barely has a story, but hurtling through the darkness of space has entertained guests around the world for over forty years! In this case, the emotion evoked through this minimalist design is one of having survived something outside of one's comfort zone. Disney Legend John Hench loved telling the story of observing a group of guests exiting the ride, falling to the ground, and declaring, "I feel so alive! I feel so alive!" Again, you won't get that reaction if you don't start with a reassuring design.

MK: What role do sensory triggers play in creating an immersive experience?

BV: Sensory triggers play a crucial role in creating a deeply immersive experience. By engaging multiple senses, participants are more likely to become fully absorbed in the environment. For example, specific smells can evoke strong memories and emotions, while sound can set the mood and reinforce the narrative. Visual details and tactile elements add to the realism and authenticity of the experience. By carefully integrating these sensory triggers, designers can create a more holistic and impactful experience that resonates with participants on multiple levels.

MK: How important is interactivity in an immersive experience?

BV: It's vital because it gives participants a sense of agency and control. When participants can influence the outcome or navigate the experience in their own way, they become more engaged and invested. Interactive elements encourage exploration, curiosity, and personal connection. This can be achieved through hands-on activities, decision-making opportunities, and personalized interactions. The goal is to make participants feel like active contributors rather than passive observers, which enhances their overall engagement and satisfaction.

However, there is something to be said about relinquishing control. We all have to make many decisions throughout the day, so it feels refreshing to give that control to someone else for a moment. Think about going on a favorite thrill ride in a Disney theme park, like Indiana Jones Adventure. The guest actually relinquishes their agency the moment they decide to sit in the ride vehicle and buckle up and it starts to move. But that isn't a good story. A good story is "Don't anger the ancient gods." That happens in the first scene of the attraction when we're told not to look in the eye of Mara, an ancient god believed to be protecting the temple. Of course, the ride will continue as designed whether a guest looks into the eye of Mara or not, but the setup is so playful that guests either believe someone did look or don't care because it's a fun moment of anticipation. The moment of surrendering agency is felt by all to be the moment Mara has been disobeyed.

MK: How do you think about gameplay in an immersive experience or theme park setting?

BV: Gameplay is often a secondary design element in a theme park. The primary areas of focus are emotion and perception. How do you evoke the strongest emotions, and how do you create a believable perception or suspension of disbelief in your guests? For example, in Toy Story Midway Mania!, guests are playing a shoot-the-target game in a digital format, but in the context of a story world. The story is that if the toys all came together and constructed their own boardwalk games, what would it look like? They would use other toys and objects around them to create the gameplay. So you have the emotion of connecting with your favorite characters in your favorite story world, but you're also believing that you are shooting targets in the context of the *Toy Story* world.

Midway games may or may not be fun, but playing a midway game with your favorite characters sure is!

MK: What are you excited about in the future of immersive storytelling?
BV: I'm looking forward to seeing the future of XR, extended reality, glasses in immersive experiences. Something I could wear to experience a dimensional world around me. Something I could wear that's not a bother, where the benefits outweigh the inconvenience. After all, it's only in the last twenty years or so that most people started carrying cell phones. Growing up, I never thought I'd be carrying a personal computer with me everywhere I go. Now my iPhone is like one of my organs! Glasses seems like something that most people would accept. I'm looking forward to seeing where that goes. We can really up the ante on making magic when we can design mixed-reality theme park environments.

"It is not the critic who counts: not the man who points out how the strong man stumbles or where the doer of deeds could have done better. The credit belongs to the man who is actually in the arena, whose face is marred by dust and sweat and blood, who strives valiantly, who errs and comes up short again and again, because there is no effort without error or shortcoming, but who knows the great enthusiasms, the great devotions, who spends himself in a worthy cause; who, at the best, knows, in the end, the triumph of high achievement, and who, at the worst, if he fails, at least he fails while daring greatly, so that his place shall never be with those cold and timid souls who knew neither victory nor defeat."

— THEODORE ROOSEVELT, "THE MAN IN THE ARENA,"
PARIS, APRIL 23, 1910

12

TO THOSE IN THE ARENA

||||||||||||||||||||||||||||||||||||||||||||||||||||||||||||||||||||||||||||||||||||||||||||||||||||||||||||||

I DEATING, DESIGNING, AND MAKING any form of storytelling is one of the most challenging tasks we could ever embark on as creative beings. The road is treacherous, unpredictable, and far from ordinary. You will encounter naysayers and nonbelievers who will immediately respond to your suggestions with "that's a terrible idea," "that won't work," "that's impossible," "we can't do that," and "that's not how we do things around here."

I think the lesson all of us as creatives and writers should learn is that you simply need to have the courage to do it. To take the risk, make the big leap, fail fast, fail often, get up, brush yourself off, and try again. This is not a line of work for the fainthearted. It's hard, grueling work that requires tenacity, resilience, passion, and drive. You need moxie: a courageous spirit and determination. You need to hone your ability to listen to the right people. You don't take no for an answer. Instead you hear: "Not right now." Or "Not for me." So you find someone else, who'll say, "Yes, right now. And yes, with me."

You love working with other people. You love working in teams. In fact, you get energy from it. Because together, you'll be facing the arena. You'll work together and have each other's backs. Together, you'll go through bad ideas, brutal feedback, lack of resources and funding, operational challenges, hundreds of iterations, installations, and hours upon hours of production work.

Then you open your work to the world. That's all you can do. Let it go and share it. Your baby is all grown up. And you hope, with all of your heart, that you've done everything you can to make sure that everyone will love it as much as you do. You'll be so proud of that work and the people who helped it get there. You cry. You celebrate.

And the next day, if you're fortunate enough, you get to do it all over again.

People will criticize your work. Say that you missed this and that. That you should've done this and that. That it's no good or could be better. But guess what? You were the one who bled, sweated, and teared. They weren't. You created something out of nothing. You were the creator. You ARE a creator.

Creators support other creators. We stand by them, we raise them up, and we celebrate them. Either you're in the arena or you're not. Either you play the game or you don't. We don't talk about doing it. We do it.

To all those who are actually in the arena and who dare greatly, I salute you. I am proud of your work, and I can't wait to experience what you create. Thank you for all that you do. Keep creating amazing things. Keep making the magic. Keep sharing your stories. Keep giving us every reason to play.

I'll see you in the arena.

ACKNOWLEDGMENTS

||||||||||||||||||||||||||||||||||||||||||||||||||||||||||||||||||||||||||||||||||||

This book would not have been possible without the relentless support of Geraldine Overton, Alexander Ward, and Ken Lee of Michael Wiese Productions. You entrusted me to share my wisdom in my first book, *Immersive Storytelling for Real and Imagined Worlds*, and have entrusted me again to share my insights in this book. Thank you to my talented editor, Karen Krumpak, for bringing much-needed cohesion and reorganization to this work. Much gratitude to the late Michael Wiese for giving us creatives and writers the opportunity to stand up, speak up, and share our ideas with the world. You have left us a legacy that will live on forever.

Thank you to Bruce Vaughn, Amber Samdahl, Wendy McClellan Anderson, Kamal Sinclair, Todd Martens, and Joe Rohde for sharing your insights with me. Thank you to Jeanne Normand Goswami, editor of the *Exhibition* journal, for my interview article.

Bryce, thank you for coming into my life. You give me every reason to keep pushing myself so that I can show you that anything is possible if you dream it and put in the hard work. Thank you for reminding me there's always time to play. I love being your mama, and I love you more than you'll ever know.

Thank you to my husband Foster. I can never thank you enough. You are the reason I can be a writer on top of being a wife, a mother, and a full-time employee. Thank you for making sure our household doesn't fall apart. Thank you for supporting me in all of my nutty endeavors. Thank you for your endless patience. Thank you for being the best dad. Thank you for being the best partner in life.

Finally, thank you to my readers. Thank you for buying my books, coming to my presentations, and supporting all of my endeavors. You fuel me to keep writing and sharing. Thank you for all of your positive feedback, and your questions, and for sharing your support of my books via social media. Please keep sharing them. I love seeing how I can be a part of supporting your creative endeavors.

APPENDIX A:
JUMP-STARTER QUESTIONS

Here's a list of questions to help jump-start your writing through the lens of a gamer. Make sure you have answers to all of these questions before you start designing your experience. Don't worry. These answers can change and evolve as you iterate on your project. Nothing is set in stone.

1. What is your story about? In other words, what's the theme?
2. Why is your story set in this world? What is the world you're creating? Consider the mood, tone, and genre.
3. Who is your participant? What role are they going to play in your experience? How will you meet them where they are? Will they want to be a part of your story?
4. Have you captured the 6 Es of Great Storytelling in Games? Is your experience engaging, educational, emotional, experimental, exploratory, and evergreen?
5. When will you playtest your experience with an audience, receive their feedback, and reiterate? Plan for it.
6. How will you give agency to your participant? What is the gameplay of your experience? At what points will you give them choices to make?
7. How will you immerse the participant in all of their senses?
8. What is the guest flow? How will they physically experience your story?
9. What is the guest promise? What's their wish fulfillment?
10. What will be your visitor's first cue that they're about to enter a new world?

11. What narrative style best suits your visitors' engagement with your experience? How do the gameplay and story support one another?

12. What emotional takeaway does your experience aim to convey, and how do the audience's actions contribute to that meaning?

13. What are the consequences in your experience, and how will they be FELT by the participant?

14. What will make your experience successful as a standalone, regardless of familiarity with the subject matter or story?

15. What are the pacing and tension of the experience? How will you design and control these elements?

16. Who are the NPCs (nonplayable characters) in your experience, and WHY are they there?

17. How will each participant engage with the others, if any others are present?

18. Are there different levels to unlock? Are there rewards and achievements?

19. Are there elements of collaboration or competition? If so, where and how?

20. What industries, topics, or stories do you care about deeply? What new immersive experiences can you envision for these interests?

21. What new understanding and questions about their own world do you hope your visitors take away from your experience?

APPENDIX B: PREVISUALIZATION STORYTELLING TOOLS

||||||||||||||||||||||||||||||||||||||||||||||||||||||||||||||||||||||||||||||||||||||||||||

There isn't any RIGHT way to start creating the design of your experience. My advice is to start with a process that excites you, a process that you're familiar with and can stick to for days and weeks to come. The following are some suggestions on how to previsualize and start gathering your thoughts to further hone your concept.

CREATE A DESIGN DECK

If you're a whiz at building Keynote or PowerPoint presentations, then you can start to visualize your idea slide by slide. Keep it to one thought or idea per slide. Here's an example template:

Slide 1: Title and intro
Slide 2: What's the big idea/theme?
Slide 3: What's the guest promise?
Slide 4: What's the participant's role?
Slide 5: What's the gameplay?
Slide 6: What's the setting/world?
Slide 7: What are the main story points?
Slide 8: Who (if anyone) will they meet?
Slide 9: What's the emotional takeaway?

WRITE A STORY OUTLINE OR BEAT SHEET

All you need is a notebook or Word document to create your story beat by beat. You can create a story outline based on a first-person perspective of your participant. Start at the very first scene and build each subsequent scene to describe what your participant encounters, sees, and does. What are the choices they have to make? Who will they meet? Keep writing without editing yourself. You can edit later, but the first draft is always terrible for everyone. Simply let your ideas flow out of you onto paper or screen without the critical editorial voice. You may find some gems worth keeping later in the process.

DRAW A BRANCHING NARRATIVE DIAGRAM

You might be more visual and want to create a flowchart or decision tree diagram to show the progression of your story. You can do this with paper notecards that you tape on your wall or use a software that helps you create narrative "branches" based on your participant's decisions. This is a really great way to see the bigger picture of your experience based on the actions of your participant.

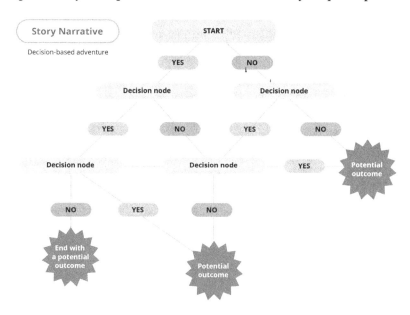

BUILD A BOARD GAME

Another effective way to visualize your experience is by creating a simple board game. What key features and moves would convey the story in this 2D form? Not only is it fun to make, but you can iterate easily using a whiteboard or some other medium like a sketch tool on your tablet or a large piece of paper. This is also an easy way to playtest your experience with family and friends. Playing board games is familiar to most people, so there's not much of a learning curve. They can focus on the story and gameplay at hand.

CREATE STORY CARDS

Using index cards, write or draw each step of your participant's journey. Start with the setting on the first card and continue step-by-step until you've written or drawn out every scene and decision point for your participant. When you playtest with a friend, have them sit across from you, and "play out" the experience by revealing the next story card or decision card that they have chosen. Place the card on the table and continue playing until the end of the game.

For example:

Card 1: Welcome to "Otherside," an alternate dimension.

Card 2: You wake up and find yourself alone in an empty room.

Card 3: There are two doors. Which do you choose to open? Left or right?

Card 4: You open the left door and step inside.

Card 5: You enter what looks like a kitchen from the 1980s.

Card 6: There's a woman looking out of the window at someone or something.

Card 7: Do you approach her? Or do you walk out of the kitchen to the garden?

Card 8: And so on. . .

You can choose to draw one image or write only a few words on the card while narrating the rest of the story orally, setting up the environment, and immersing your player in your world. Or you can choose to have your player physically walk around the room or your house and perform actions based on their decisions. It's up to you to make the experience as immersive as possible.

BUILD YOUR WORLD

As a child, I used felt, paper, clay, toys, sticks, mud, and other materials to create my worlds. I drew out architectural layouts of buildings and spaces that my characters would inhabit and play in. Similar to when creating a board game, I wanted to visualize my worlds in different formats. I wanted to feel them in my hands and create something physical that my subconscious mind would help me manifest.

If you're a painter, paint your world. If you enjoy playing with clay, mold out the world and don't worry about how rough it looks. Simply be open to the act of creation and self-expression. You'll be surprised as to what you'll come up with by using various mediums and by engaging your hands in different materials.

The best part is that if you don't like it, you can squash it or throw it away. By creating a small model of your world, you can envision what it looks and feels like without investing too much energy or resources. The act of creativity begins with jumping into the practice and experimenting and exploring. If you're constantly looking at a screen to create, you're limiting yourself to one kind of creative expression. Be open to practicing your creativity in other forms and you won't be disappointed.

APPENDIX C: CONSIDERATIONS FOR CREATING AN ENGAGING GUEST JOURNEY

I mentioned playing the first-person perspective video game *Gone Home* and how time seemed to fly by. I was in the moment and felt a sense of urgency that was delivered by the game's ability to master its pacing and tension. Designing a game shares many similarities to writing a physical immersive experience. There are techniques that can be used to maintain a perfect balance of tension and release, keeping players and participants engaged throughout their journey. When you apply these principles to your writing, you ensure your audiences are hooked from start to finish. You give them a compelling and meaningful guest flow.

Here are some ways to create an engaging guest journey.

VARY THE INTENSITY

As in life, there are peaks and valleys in storytelling. Alternate between moments of intense action and quieter, more contemplative moments, especially when the scene calls for it. This variation keeps players on their toes and provides a sense of rhythm. It's also a good reminder for a breather if the prior scene was very intense, giving your participant a moment to reflect and collect themselves physically and mentally.

"TICKING TIME BOMB"

Introduce unique timed challenges or objectives that create a sense of urgency. Players feel compelled to make quick decisions, enhancing tension and engagement. Consider how you can make the time pressure dependent on teamwork and collaboration, between friends and strangers alike. The escape room model is a perfect example.

LEVEL UP

Start with relatively simple challenges and gradually ramp up the difficulty. This allows your participants to build their confidence while keeping them engaged as they face progressively tougher obstacles. This also allows your participants to engage more as they progress; as they become more comfortable with the world and gameplay, they move from passive observer to active participant.

BRANCHING NARRATIVES

Offer branching storylines or choices that lead to different outcomes. Participants become more invested when they feel their decisions impact the narrative, encouraging them to explore multiple paths. Even if certain branches don't directly impact the narrative, they may offer visibility to a scene or gameplay that other participants on other branches may have missed.

The Willows by JFI Productions is a great example of bringing participants into different scenes to experience something different from the other participants. Certain scenes bring participants together (e.g., the dinner, the dance, card games), but some participants are taken in other directions, all within the story of the world. It's an innovative take on the "murder mystery dinner theatre."[36]

---

[36] https://thewillowsla.com/

GOOD THINGS COME TO THOSE WHO WAIT

Foreshadowing is a great tool. Drop subtle hints or foreshadowing about future events to build anticipation and curiosity among participants. This could potentially create a satisfying aha! emotional payoff when the participant realizes that the answer was in front of them all along.

You can also introduce a delayed reward system in which participants have to invest time and effort before receiving a satisfying payoff. This can create a sense of anticipation and keep participants engaged in the pursuit of the reward. The trick here is to make sure that the payoff is worth it. Whether the payoff is emotional, such as a satisfying end to the story, or physical, where they receive an object or item, it has to feel proportional to the effort that they have put into your experience.

KEEP THEM GUESSING

Start with a strong narrative hook that immediately captures the participants' attention and makes them curious about the story's direction. Don't underestimate your participants' need to make sense of things and solve all of the mysteries and puzzles. Present unresolved mysteries or unanswered questions early on. They will be motivated to continue playing to uncover the answers, maintaining their interest and engagement. As the game progresses, evolve the objectives or goals, introducing new elements that keep players engaged and motivated to continue. Incorporate unexpected and unpredictable events, surprises, or plot twists. These can catch participants off guard, heightening tension and curiosity about what will happen next.

CHARACTERS TO ROOT FOR

There's no better way to keep participants engaged than by having them connect with characters they have met along the way.

Develop relatable, well-rounded characters with personal goals and conflicts. Participants will become emotionally invested in their stories, increasing engagement as they root for their success. By introducing emotionally charged moments with the characters, your participants receive cues on how to FEEL, eliciting strong emotions and enhancing their connection to the narrative.

RICH ENVIRONMENTS

Similar to richly designed game environments, use the world itself to tell a story. Scatter clues, hints, and lore throughout the environment, encouraging participants to explore and discover more narrative details. This also helps to increase the replay value of your experience, encouraging visitors to return again and again to uncover more elements.

SEE, HEAR, TOUCH, SMELL

Utilize audio and visual cues to signal changes in pacing or imminent threats. Heightened music or changes in lighting can build tension and alert participants to upcoming challenges. *Sleep No More* does this very effectively, as participants are encouraged to move around different scenes with the aid of lighting and music so they will encounter the major plot points. Perhaps you can even use temperature changes, water, and other natural elements like light fog to create a pathway, to encourage or discourage participants from a certain option. Is there a smell that can invite or divert your participants from a certain area?

FEEDBACK MECHANISMS

In some immersive experiences, I feel like there should be some way for me to ask someone "Am I doing this right?" Sometimes we need to receive and give feedback based on our performance. This is done effectively in some escape rooms when we get stuck on a problem and can ask a question to the live host or the operator watching us. Also, the time I got stuck in *The Nest* with a particular challenge, I picked up a physical phone and talked to the Operator. In addition to being a "voice from above" or a physical object, these feedback mechanisms could come in the form of visual cues, audio cues, and more, as long as they acknowledge and celebrate the visitor's progress, achievements, and next steps.

All of these storytelling techniques (or a combination of them) are dependent on the genre and the style of your game, as well as the specific experience you want to create. Experimenting with different approaches to pacing and tension will help you find the right balance to hook and captivate your participant effectively.

INDEX OF GAMES

INDEX OF PLACES AND EXPERIENCES

ABOUT THE AUTHOR

Born in Indonesia and raised in Singapore, Margaret has built a career spanning over sixteen years of creating narratives and writing for television, film, digital media, games, brand storytelling, location-based entertainment, narrative placemaking, and immersive experiences. She is a Narrative Lead, Story Consultant, and Writer for multiple award-winning projects around the world, including *Star Wars*: Galaxy's Edge, the *Star Wars*: Batuu Bounty Hunters augmented reality mobile game, *Star Wars*: Rise of the Resistance, National Geographic Base Camp, and the NASA Kennedy Space Center Visitor Complex. She was a Disney Imagineer from 2014 to 2021. She is the author of *Immersive Storytelling for Real and Imagined Worlds: A Writer's Guide* (2022) and *Reimagined Worlds: Narrative Placemaking for People, Play, and Purpose* (2024). Margaret was the 2023 Paul Helmle Fellow for the Department of Architecture at California Polytechnic State University, Pomona. She is currently living in Los Angeles with her husband and son and is always looking for her next adventure and invitation to play.

THE WRITER'S JOURNEY
MYTHIC STRUCTURE FOR WRITERS

25TH ANNIVERSARY EDITION

CHRISTOPHER VOGLER

Originally an influential memo Vogler wrote for Walt Disney Animation executives regarding *The Lion King, The Writer's Journey* details a twelve-stage, myth-inspired method that has galvanized Hollywood's treatment of cinematic storytelling. A format that once seldom deviated beyond a traditional three-act blueprint, Vogler's comprehensive theory of story structure and character development has met with universal acclaim, and is detailed herein using examples from myths, fairy tales, and classic movies. This book has changed the face of screenwriting worldwide over the last 25 years, and continues to do so.

"This book is like having the smartest person in the story meeting come home with you and whisper what to do in your ear as you write a screenplay. Insight for insight, step for step, Chris Vogler takes us through the process of connecting theme to story and making a script come alive."
  — Lynda Obst, producer, *How to Lose a Guy in 10 Days, Sleepless in Seattle, One Fine Day, Contact*; author, *Hello, He Lied*

"The Writer's Journey is an insightful and even inspirational guide to the craft of storytelling. An approach to structure that is fresh and contemporary, while respecting our roots in mythology."
  — Charles Russell, writer, director, producer, *Dreamscape, The Mask, Eraser*

"The Writer's Journey should be on anyone's bookshelf who cares about the art of storytelling at the movies. Not just some theoretical tome filled with development clichés of the day, this book offers sound and practical advice on how to construct a story that works."
  — David Friendly, producer, *Little Miss Sunshine, Daylight, Courage Under Fire, Out to Sea, My Girl*

CHRISTOPHER VOGLER made documentary films as an Air Force officer before studying film production at the University of Southern California, where he encountered the ideas of mythologist Joseph Campbell and observed how they influenced the story design of 1977's *Star Wars*. He worked as a story consultant in the development departments of 20th Century Fox, Walt Disney Pictures and Animation, and Paramount Pictures, and wrote an influential memo on Campbell's Hero's Journey concept that led to his involvement in Disney's *Aladdin, The Lion King*, and *Hercules*. After the publication of *The Writer's Journey*, he developed stories for many productions, including Disney's remake of *101 Dalmatians*, Fox's *Fight Club, Courage Under Fire, Volcano*, and *The Thin Red Line*.

$29.95 · 400 PAGES · ISBN: 9781615933150

IMMERSIVE STORYTELLING FOR REAL AND IMAGINED WORLDS:
A WRITER'S GUIDE

MARGARET KERRISON

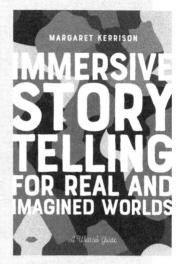

Welcome to the new world of immersive storytelling.

What gets your heart rate going more: reading a story about dinosaurs, or being chased by one? The emerging discipline of immersive storytelling recognizes the power of creative works that put the viewer at the center of the action. In *Immersive Storytelling*, theme park designer Margaret Kerrison shares tips and tricks for writers on teams tasked with bringing a narrative to life. How do you take an idea from inspiration to manifestation? How do you move from telling a story to creating a world?

In this richly illustrated book—the first of its kind written specifically for writers—Kerrison lays out the craft of immersive storytelling. She uses case studies to show what works, and highlights the essential role of the writer on a complex creative team. Ready to take the kernel of an idea and turn it into a full-fledged experience? This book gives you the blueprint.

"The communal wisdom, experience, and real-world examples collected here represent a career's worth of exposure. Immerse yourself."
 —Joe Rohde, Veteran Executive of Walt Disney Imagineering

"Margaret's belief is that the personal can be universal, and invites all of us, regardless of ethnicity, nationality, or gender to investigate why the stories we want to tell matter."
 —Shelby Jiggetts-Tivony, VP. Creative & Advanced Development, Disney Live Entertainment

"Immersive storytelling in themed environments is an evolving, audience-driven, and play-focused medium that has lacked serious, practical, and conversational dissection. Until now."
 —Todd Martens, theme park journalist for the *Los Angeles Times*

MARGARET KERRISON was born in Indonesia and raised in Singapore, Margaret received her Master of Fine Arts degree in Screenwriting from the University of Southern California School of Cinematic Arts. Her career spans 14 years of experience in television, film, digital media, games, brand storytelling, location-based entertainment, and immersive experiences. She has worked as a Story Lead, Story Consultant, and Writer for multiple projects around the world, including *Star Wars: Galaxy's Edge, Star Wars: Launch Bay, Star Wars: Galactic Starcruiser, Avengers Campus, Guardians of the Galaxy: Cosmic Rewind, National Geographic HQ*, and the NASA Kennedy Space Center Visitor Complex's *Journey to Mars: Explorers Wanted*. She was a Disney Imagineer from 2014-2021. She is currently a Sr. Experiential Creative Lead for Airbnb.

$22.46 · 264 PAGES · ORDER #246RLS · ISBN 9781615933419

SAVE THE CAT!®
THE LAST BOOK ON SCREENWRITING YOU'LL EVER NEED!

BLAKE SNYDER

BEST SELLER

He's made millions of dollars selling screenplays to Hollywood and now screenwriter Blake Snyder tells all. "Save the Cat!®" is just one of Snyder's many ironclad rules for making your ideas more marketable and your script more satisfying — and saleable, including:
- The four elements of every winning logline.
- The seven immutable laws of screenplay physics.
- The 10 genres and why they're important to your movie.
- Why your Hero must serve your idea.
- Mastering the Beats.
- Mastering the Board to create the Perfect Beast.
- How to get back on track with ironclad and proven rules for script repair.

This ultimate insider's guide reveals the secrets that none dare admit, told by a show biz veteran who's proven that you can sell your script if you can save the cat.

"Imagine what would happen in a town where more writers approached screenwriting the way Blake suggests? My weekend read would dramatically improve, both in sellable/producible content and in discovering new writers who understand the craft of storytelling and can be hired on assignment for ideas we already have in house."
> – From the Foreword by Sheila Hanahan Taylor, Vice President, Development at Zide/Perry Entertainment, whose films include *American Pie, Cats and Dogs, Final Destination*

"One of the most comprehensive and insightful how-to's out there. Save the Cat!® *is a must-read for both the novice and the professional screenwriter."*
> – Todd Black, Producer, *The Pursuit of Happyness, The Weather Man, S.W.A.T, Alex and Emma, Antwone Fisher*

"Want to know how to be a successful writer in Hollywood? The answers are here. Blake Snyder has written an insider's book that's informative — and funny, too."
> – David Hoberman, Producer, *The Shaggy Dog* (2005), *Raising Helen, Walking Tall, Bringing Down the House, Monk* (TV)

BLAKE SNYDER, besides selling million-dollar scripts to both Disney and Spielberg, was one of Hollywood's most successful spec screenwriters. Blake's vision continues on *www.blakesnyder.com*.

$20.95 · 216 PAGES · ORDER NUMBER 34RLS · ISBN: 9781932907001

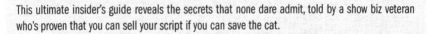

© MICHELE MONTEZ

MICHAEL WIESE PRODUCTIONS

I N A DARK TIME, a light bringer came along, leading the curious and the frustrated to clarity and empowerment. It took the well-guarded secrets out of the hands of the few and made them available to all. It spread a spirit of openness and creative freedom, and built a storehouse of knowledge dedicated to the betterment of the arts.

The essence of Michael Wiese Productions (MWP) is empowering people who have the burning desire to express themselves creatively. We help them realize their dreams by putting the tools in their hands. We demystify the sometimes secretive worlds of screenwriting, directing, acting, producing, film financing, and other media crafts.

By doing so, we hope to bring forth a realization of 'conscious media,' which we define as being positively charged, emphasizing hope, and affirming positive values like trust, cooperation, self-empowerment, freedom, and love. Grounded in the deep roots of myth, it aims to be healing both for those who make the art and those who encounter it. It hopes to be transformative for people, opening doors to new possibilities and pulling back veils to reveal hidden worlds.

MWP has built a storehouse of knowledge unequaled in the world, for no other publisher has so many titles on the media arts. Please visit www.mwp.com, where you will find many free resources and a 25% discount on our books. Sign up and become part of the wider creative community!

MICHAEL WIESE, Co-Publisher
GERALDINE OVERTON, Co-Publisher

mw